SAY WHAT?

THE FICTION WRITER'S HANDY GUIDE TO GRAMMAR, PUNCTUATION, AND WORD USAGE

C. S. LAKIN

SAY WHAT?: THE FICTION WRITER'S HANDY GUIDE TO GRAMMAR, PUNCTUATION, AND WORD USAGE BY C. S. LAKIN

Copyright©2014 by C. S. Lakin

Cover and interior designed by Ellie Searl, Publishista®

ISBN-10: 0991389409

ISBN-13: 978-0-9913894-0-7

LCCN: 2014931333

UBIQUITOUS PRESS

Boulder Creek, CA

"Good, concise and easily accessible reference books on grammar and usage is hard to find. I mean, *are* hard to find. This is one of them."

~ James Scott Bell, writing coach, and author of REVISION AND SELF-EDITING FOR PUBLICATION

"This handy, user-friendly reference book, presented with style and humor, is a must for any writer serious about honing their craft and garnering respect for their works. An essential resource, the e-book will save you time with all its quick links to the short, snappy topics, and the print version is small enough to stay within reach beside your computer, so I highly recommend getting both. Respected editor and writer C. S. Lakin succeeds in making a dry topic interesting and meaningful! And using this book will also help you reduce your editing costs."

~ Jodie Renner, editor, and author of STYLE THAT SIZZLES

"As a self-professed grammar nerd, let me just say this: The world needs more grammar nerds. Editor Lakin is doing her part to make this happen with her pithy, fun, and supremely useful guide to the everyday writing mistakes most of us don't even realize we're making. Her book is conversational and approachable enough to make for enjoyable reading. But its true value is in its 'lookupability.' This is the perfect guide to keep on your desk, next to your computer, for those moments when you're just not sure which word is right."

~ K. M. Weiland, author of STRUCTURING YOUR NOVEL and OUTLINING YOUR NOVEL

CONTENTS

CONTENTS

CONTENTS

CONTENTS

CONTENTS

PREFACE

FICTION WRITERS, WHEN IN THE throes of creativity and busily working away on their story, don't want to interrupt "the flow" by stopping and searching for grammar help online or thumbing through a stack of books. If they need an answer to a puzzling problem, they'd like the answer quickly—so they can get back to writing. And they'd like the answer to be simple to understand. There are few things more intimidating to a fiction writer than a litany of the names of the parts of speech and the usages thereof. Who has the time (or interest) to memorize all those terms—such as "nominal clause" and "past perfect indicative"—and exactly what they mean? Yet, writers do need to have a good grasp of the English language (if they write in English) and understand the basics of proper grammar, punctuation, and usage. There's just no getting around it.

For years I've kept a notebook by my desk, and every time I researched a grammar question and found the answer I needed, I jotted it in my notebook. Although I tried to enter these in some kind of order, it was inevitable that my notes would end up in a haphazard mess. I thought that one day I would type them all into a document so I could organize them, but that seemed tedious and a waste of time. So I kept scribbling, and when I needed to find that grammar rule again, I would thumb through my notebook, which was growing more and more disorganized the longer it got.

Why couldn't someone put out a handy guide to grammar that I could keep at my desk, and that would organize the mess for me? I wondered. Hence, the idea for my blog column *Say What?* and the compilation of the first three years' posts into that handy guide.

If you're like me and have a colander-type brain, you'll look up the same things over and over and wonder why the rule just won't stick (like a good starchy noodle to the side of a colander). Even the smartest, most experienced editor will still have to check the same rules again and again. So, since most of us don't have perfect memories (and aren't trained as copyeditors), having this guide to grammar at hand might be the next best thing.

Although this handy guide covers most of the grammar, punctuation, and usage issues you come across as you write, you may find some others that aren't included. To help you keep all your notes in one place (and not end up with the mess I did), extra blank pages are provided at the end of each section for you to scribble these down.

Here's what I recommend: Get both the print version and the ebook version of this book. Why?

First: You can keep the print book at your side when you write or edit your book, story, or memoir and the ebook accessible on your computer (using something like the free Kindle Cloud reader) so you can call up the book and do quick, easy searches anywhere you're working, anywhere in the world. You don't even need an Internet connection once you download the book into your "library."

Second: From time to time, more posts will be added to the ebook via updated versions, which you will get for free. Amazon notifies you when these versions are available, so while your print book won't automatically update (I'm waiting for that technology!), over time you will have more entries in your ebook. Eventually the print book will move into newer editions with those added entries.

Now you won't have to let those nagging grammar questions interrupt your creativity anymore!

A WORD ABOUT GRAMMAR AND FICTION

In my work as a full-time copyeditor and writing coach, I critique and edit more than two hundred partial or complete manuscripts a year, from clients in six continents. That's a lot of diverse writing I examine, in just about every genre. But although these works are very different from each other, I see time and again many of the same grammar and sentence structure mistakes. The same words appear again and again misspelled or misused. It became clear after perusing so many manuscripts which mistakes were the most common and sorely needed addressing.

Not all questions about grammar are simple, and often there are gray areas and situations that are matters of style. This becomes an even greater component when dealing with fiction, which introduces elements of characterization, regional speech, and creative writing style.

Most writers want to "follow the rules" of grammar, yet don't want their style encroached upon. However, the more a fiction writer knows and understands the rules of grammar, the better equipped she will be to write well—and to make sound decisions regarding when or if to break the "rules."

Some writers feel they don't need to bother with becoming proficient in grammar and proper word usage; that's the job of a copyeditor, and they can just hire one to clean up all the "mess" that's in their manuscript. It's true—messy manuscripts keep copyeditors busy. But aside from the obvious reason for becoming a proficient handler of language (you're a writer, after all, and language is the tool of your craft), learning grammar will make your job easier and your writing much better in the long run. And those are goals, it seems, most writers would embrace and strive for.

Since you've bought this book, it stands to reason that you have a desire to learn. To become a better writer—a more proficient handler of the English language. If that's the case, don't just use this handy guide when you're stumped on a grammar question. Why not read one entry a day, then try to apply what you learned by writing some sentences in your current work in progress that use the words or rules? Practice moves concepts into your long-term memory, making what you learn available to draw on in the future.

In addition to general grammar and usage rules, I've included dozens of fiction tips drawn from what I've observed in the manuscripts I critique as well as numerous insights from successful authors.

My aim in compiling this guide is to help you write the beautiful novels and stories you yearn to tell—and to tell them in your own unique style while skillfully wielding language so that you will say what you mean and don't say what you don't mean. Learning the craft of writing includes learning correct grammar, spelling, punctuation, and word usage, but it shouldn't painful or boring. I hope by providing these short and easy-to-understand entries drawn from the Say What? section of Live Write Thrive (www.livewritethrive.com), you'll actually enjoy the process.

Happy writing!

~ C. S. Lakin

GRAMMAR

I LIKE THIS SIMPLE DEFINITION OF *grammar*. "The study of how words and their component parts combine to form sentences" (www.thefreedictionary.com). Grammar is all about words, and words can often be tricky things to wield. If we put a word in the wrong place in a sentence, it might completely change the meaning of that sentence. Nouns and verbs have to agree, and we don't want anything dangling where it shouldn't be. Heaven forbid if we misplace a modifier.

Sometimes we don't see what's wrong with a sentence, and that's why it's important to take the time to study some of the basic rules of grammar and learn about some of the common pitfalls writers fall into.

We don't want to be like this person Carl Sandburg wrote about: "I never made a mistake in grammar but one in my life and as soon as I done it I seen it."

Learning the English language is hard. As columnist and editor Doug Larson said: "If the English language made any sense, a catastrophe would be an apostrophe with fur."

But, as we writers well know, sometimes (if not often) language rules don't make sense. Yet, we are expected to learn and apply grammar rules to our writing so that it is correctly structured—unless we deliberately break the rules for some reason. And you know that wise saying about breaking the rules: "You have to know the rules before you can break them."

In fiction, there is a time and place to break grammar rules, but those should be intentional—not a result of ignorance. Try to think of grammar rules as friends that help you along in your writing journey. Good friends support you and help you reach your goals. Good grammar will do likewise with your writing.

"English is a funny language; that explains why we park our car on the driveway and drive our car on the parkway."

~ Anonymous

"You write to communicate to the hearts and minds of others what's burning inside you. And we edit to let the fire show through the smoke."

~ Arthur Polotnik

SPELLING

A WORD ABOUT DUMB SPELL-CHECKERS

I'm of the opinion we should do away with spell-checkers. For one thing, they're a bit like calculators (except flawed). Remember when you had to actually learn and memorize your multiplication tables? Anyone recall how to do long division? Oh-no! What do you do if your smartphone dies at the restaurant and you have no way to calculate the 15% tip? Boy, will you be in trouble.

Okay . . . I'm sure I made my point. What's so wrong about learning how to spell well? Sure, even the smartest and most learned have to look up the spelling of a word on occasion (unless you're a national spelling bee champion, but those people study the dictionary, like, eight hours a day). And another thing: spell-checkers are often just plain wrong. To me, it's like giving the kid with the D in English the job of correcting everyone's spelling. Say what?

Run this sentence through your spell-checker: "The ideal candidate will *posses* great charisma." Your checker will not catch the misspelling of *posses*, which, to it, is the plural of *posse*. Spell-checkers don't get grammar, and they can't think. Really.

Sure, you can catch some mistakes with your spell-checker, but please don't rely on it to do a thorough and accurate job. Spend some time and learn how to spell. Study grammar. You want to be a great writer? Be a great speller while you're at it. Learn how to conjugate verbs correctly. All the effort you put out to master your language can only help you in the long run to be a stronger writer. Enough said.

Now, enjoy this poem that shows why you might need a human proofreader to correct your writing (author anonymous):

I have a lovely spelling check
That came with my PC,
Witch plainly marks, four my revue,
Miss takes I can not sea.
I've run this poem threw the thing.
I'm sure your please too no.
It's latter perfect in every weigh.
My checker tolled me sew.

Happy righting!

CHOPPING OFF WORDS TO MAKE THEM TASTE GOOD

I'm fascinated with the fluidity of language and how every day it seems words come and go around us. Think how over time we have dropped the last letter or two off certain nouns—perhaps just out of carelessness or due to our verbally dropping them (and just not hearing them in speech) such that over time the acceptable spelling of these words changed. Here are some words as they were originally penned:

- panned cakes (pancakes)
- iced tea (that's the correct form, but we say "ice tea" much of the time)
- powered steering
- linked sausages (makes more sense, doesn't it?)
- creamed cheese (same here)
- roasted beef

Maybe over time some of these (and many other) words will be shortened even further, as we continue to chop up our language via text messaging. Now even phrases are shortened into acronyms to save time typing (like ROFL and LOL, which I use a lot. If you don't know what these mean, ask someone who texts a lot). We now put chops on the barbie and drink (soda) pop and eat dogs. Seems like this is really all about food, hmmm.

Maybe we're in such a rush to eat, we don't want to take the time to complete our sentences. Or we're talking with our mouths full and drop a few letters inadvertently. Something to chew on, eh?

TIP FOR FICTION WRITERS: "The difference between the right word and the almost right word is the difference between lightning and a lightning bug," so said Mark Twain. The task of a good writer is to make sure every word is the right word. Make every word count, and use a dictionary if you're not absolutely sure of a word's meaning.

ALL CONFUSED ENQUIRE HERE

You've probably seen these two words used in the same ways: *inquire* and *enquire*. So, is there a difference?

These are basically two spellings of the same word, which means to seek information about something or to conduct a formal investigation (usually when followed by "into"). The corresponding noun is *enquiry* or *inquiry*. Not surprisingly, *enquire* and *enquiry* are more common in British English, and *inquire* and *inquiry* are more common in US English. However, the *Guardian* (a British newspaper) tells writers to "use inquiry" and the *Oxford English Dictionary* seems to recognize *inquire* as the more dominant form. (My WordPress spell-checker keeps tagging *enquire* as an incorrect word, for example.)

I say "not surprisingly" because with many words there is a slight difference in preference depending on whether you are using UK or US style. I wonder how all those words got a little skewed, and I'm often amused (as I'm sure my UK counterparts are as well) when I hear on TV (or should I say "the telly"?) British speakers emphasizing words on the "wrong" syllable. For example, the word *controversy*—which "across the pond" is pronounced con-TROV-ersy.

So, you decide which word to use in the case of *enquire* and *inquire*. Just be consistent and go with the preferred word for the style of the country you are writing in (or for).

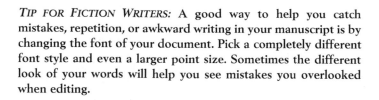

TIP FOR FICTION WRITERS: A good way to help you catch mistakes, repetition, or awkward writing in your manuscript is by changing the font of your document. Pick a completely different font style and even a larger point size. Sometimes the different look of your words will help you see mistakes you overlooked when editing.

WHO NEEDS ANY MORE TROUBLE WITH ANYMORE?

I don't want to spend any more time on this than necessary, but we should touch on *any more* and *anymore*. One word or two? That depends on what you want to communicate and if you're using British or American English.

Standard American English recognizes two distinct meanings:

Any more (two words) is an adjective phrase meaning "any additional."

- I don't want any more coffee.

Anymore is an adverb meaning "any longer" or "nowadays" or "still." It can be used in a negative sense:

- I don't drink coffee anymore.

Or a positive sense:

- Have you got anymore coffee?

Another way of thinking of the distinction between the two, according to Bryan Garner (*Modern American Usage*), is to use anymore to indicate time and any more for quantity or degree. Both are at play in this example:

- I don't drink coffee anymore because I don't need any more caffeine.

British English is more likely to identify anymore as an alternative spelling of *any more*, without acknowledging a distinction in meaning.

One final note. When you follow with the word *than*, always use the two-word *any more*.

- I don't like paying $3.50 for a cup of coffee any more than you do.

Okay, I won't bother you anymore or give you any more examples!

TIP FOR FICTION WRITERS: **Author Tracy Kidder says, "Use words wantonly and you disappear before your own eyes. Use them well and you create yourself."**

RACKED, WRECKED, OR WHAT?

Here are some pairs of words I run across in manuscripts I'm editing that get confused. One that puzzles me is the word *wracked*. I see this often in published novels as well.

If you are *racking* your brain right now, or you're *racked* with pain, then you are spelling the word correctly.

The spelling *wracked* means wrecked. It's an old variation of that word. *Wrack* can mean a rack (noun) or a type of seaweed. But it does *not* mean to suffer pain or anguish or torture, or to strain violently (rack your brain). I don't know why this word bugs me so much, but it does.

Another pair of words I see used incorrectly a lot is *lightning* and *lightening*. It should be pretty obvious that if you plan to make something lighter, you will be *lightening* it (verb). The stuff that shoots out of the sky in a storm is *lightning*.

And then there's *compliment* and *complement* (as well as *complimentary* and *complementary*). Pay attention to that easy-to-miss difference in the vowel there.

- I pay you a compliment when I see how well your shoes complement your dress.
- If I give you complimentary tickets to the game, you might compliment on my shoes just to be nice (and hope I'll give you more in the future).

TIP FOR FICTION WRITERS: Although Billy Wilder was a movie director and writer, his advice for screenwriters is just as sage for novelists: "Develop a clean line of action for your leading character. Know where you're going. The third act must build, build, build in tempo and action until the last event, then—that's it. Don't hang around. If you have a problem with the third act, the real problem is in the first act."

THE PAST HAS PASSED

Yes, I see a bit of confusion regarding *past* and *passed*. These two words are often misused, but it's not all that hard to know which to use in a sentence. If you keep in mind that *passed* is almost always a *verb*, you won't get steered wrong (but there are some exceptions, which I'll mention below).

The word *past*, though, can function in a whole lot of different ways in a sentence.

- Past can be a noun: "I miss those old movies they had in the past."
- Past can also be an adjective: "Those days are now past." Remember: adjectives modify a noun, so you would use past when you say, "All the past governors were terrible."
- Past can be a preposition: "It's half past six."
- Past can be an adverb: "The ball soared past the goalie."

When you need a verb, use *passed*. Look at the difference between these two sentences:

- The man walked past the store.
- The man passed the store.

It's easy to see why the two can get confused. But just remember the "verb" rule.

Now, of course—time to break the rules, as is so common in the English language and what makes it all so fun (sigh).

Here are some unusual usages for *passed* as a noun or adjective:

- "Don't speak ill of the passed"—this comes from the phrase "passed away."
- "A passed pawn"—a term used in chess.
- "A passed ball"—a term used in baseball.
- "A passed midshipman/fireman/surgeon"—someone who has passed a period of instruction and qualified through examination; apparently this usage arose in the Navy.

So if you used to mess these up and now are clear, good for you. Forget your past mistakes; the past has passed and is now past.

ANYONE WANT SOME FREE REINS?

I come across this from time to time: the mix-up over the homophones *rein* and *reign*. Just why is that letter G in there anyway? The word *reign* means to rule, and comes from the Latin (thirteenth century) *regnum*, hence the silent G. Not that that will really help you remember to spell the word correctly.

The word *rein* means to restrain. You rein in a horse. Similarly, you give someone free rein to do something, meaning you are loosening the restraint on them. If you've ridden a horse, you get that. You ease up on the reins and give the horse his head so he can take off. So try to picture that when you're trying to remember which rein (not *reign* or *rain*) you are freeing.

Now, why that makes me think there's a correlation to the confusion over *throne* and *thrown*, I'm not sure. But I also see writers using *thrown* as in "The king sits on the thrown." Which is wrong. But maybe getting thrown and giving the horse free rein have something to do with it. Best to keep *throne* and *reign* together and leave the horse out of the picture.

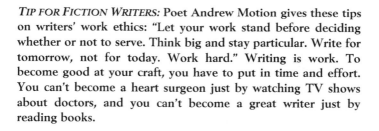

> *TIP FOR FICTION WRITERS:* Poet Andrew Motion gives these tips on writers' work ethics: "Let your work stand before deciding whether or not to serve. Think big and stay particular. Write for tomorrow, not for today. Work hard." Writing is work. To become good at your craft, you have to put in time and effort. You can't become a heart surgeon just by watching TV shows about doctors, and you can't become a great writer just by reading books.

I'D LIKE SOME TIME, ANYTIME

Writers often confuse the words *anytime* and *any time*. As is the case with *anyone* and *any one*, you need to pay attention to what you mean to say. *Anytime* means "at any time whenever." But you would use *any time* when you are talking about the noun *time*.

The same problems crop up with *sometime* (adverb or adjective) and *some time*. As with *any time*, you would use *some time* when you are speaking about the noun *time*. The following are correctly written:

- I'd like to go to the beach sometime.
- Sometime last night the burglar broke into my house.
- He's a sometime father, only coming over when he feels like it.
- I need some time to write.
- It will take some time to get over her.
- I don't have any time left in my day.
- You could see her anytime you like.

See me anytime you need some time with a friend. Sometimes that's all the time you need.

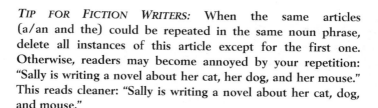

TIP FOR FICTION WRITERS: When the same articles (a/an and the) could be repeated in the same noun phrase, delete all instances of this article except for the first one. Otherwise, readers may become annoyed by your repetition: "Sally is writing a novel about her cat, her dog, and her mouse." This reads cleaner: "Sally is writing a novel about her cat, dog, and mouse."

A MATTER OF ONE LITTLE LETTER

Ever heard of a homophone? No, it's not that antique thing your grandparents played music on. Homophones are words that sound alike but are spelled differently (and hence have different meanings). Writers know how even one letter can radically change the meaning of a word, and as a result might change the entire meaning of a sentence or story. We deal with homophones all the time, for many of our English words sound alike. And perhaps because of the identical way they sound, writers can trip up and use the wrong word. Then again, some writers just might not realize they are spelling their desired word wrong.

I often see *there, they're,* and *their* mixed up. That's fairly common. I shouldn't need to explain what each means. One pair of words I also see confused are *led* and *lead.* Since the word *lead* can, in one application, be pronounced the same as *led,* many writers write lines like this:

Wrong:

- He lead the dog home.
- I lead a group on the field trip yesterday.

Another two words often confused are *born* and *borne. Born* has to do with birth, and *borne* means carried, or can be used to mean impressed. For example:

- I was born yesterday.
- I was borne by a tornado and deposited in a tree.
- It was borne upon them to vote quickly.
- He is a born optimist.

Then we have *apprise* and *appraise.* Simply put, *apprise* means to inform and *appraise* means to assess the value of.

Here are just a few more to ponder:

- Aid [meaning help] and aide [someone who assists or helps]
- Lightening [making something lighter] and lightning [that streak in the sky]
- Lose [as in lost] and loose [the opposite of tight]

Although these have a two-letter difference, *taut* and *taught* are worth noting since I also see them frequently confused. If something is tied tight, it is *taut.*

I hope I've *taught* you well.

A PEEK AT BEING PIQUED

Here's a peek into another set of homophones: *peek*, *peak*, and *pique*.

Yes—pique. Curious? You should be. That's what the verb form of *pique* means: to excite or arouse interest or anger especially by a challenge or rebuff. Or to irritate, aggravate, or to rouse resentment.

- Jennifer's curiosity was piqued when Allison hinted that she had a big announcement to make.

Pique can also be used as a noun—an offense or a transient feeling of wounded vanity.

- In a fit of pique, Eleanor stomped to her room and slammed the door.

It seems to me that quite a few people know the meaning but not the correct spelling of the word. I often see *piqued* written as *peeked* or *peaked*—both of which have only one meaning:

- Peek: a brief look, glance, or glimpse.
- Peak: top, apex, or summit. Mountains have peaks; so do careers and performances.

Example: When the hikers reached the peak of Mt. Baldy, they peeked over the top to a broad valley below.

If you're a writer, it's best to learn your peeks and peaks so you don't pique your editor.

TIP FOR FICTION WRITERS: William Faulkner said, "There is no mechanical way to get the writing done, no shortcut. The young writer would be a fool to follow a theory. Teach yourself by your own mistakes; people learn only by error." Learn from your errors and push to become a better writer.

THE PRINCIPAL PRINCIPLE

Here are two more words writers often confuse: *principal* and *principle*. *Principal* means first in authority. Or a main participant, or amount of a debt minus the interest. It can be a noun or an adjective.

Principle means a basic truth or assumption. A lot of people think of principles in relation to ethics, rules, standards, morals, guidelines, etc. It's a noun, whereas *principal* is a noun or an adjective.

If you have a lot of rules, you would have a lot of principles. If you have a weird school with more than one person in charge, you may have a number of principals. Some ballet companies have featured dancers or principals. And some principals are lacking in principles.

If you need something to help you remember when to use which spelling, think of the *pal* at the end of principal. The principal at your school should be your pal, and not be a *pill*, which is what the last syllable of *principle* sounds like (to me). Principles can feel like bitter pills. Okay, I know that's pretty dumb, but it kinda sticks, doesn't it?

TIP FOR FICTION WRITERS: Listen to what sci-fi author Michael Moorcock says: "I always advise people who want to write a fantasy or science fiction or romance to stop reading everything in those genres and start reading everything else from Bunyan to Byatt. Find an author you admire (mine was Conrad) and copy their plots and characters in order to tell your own story, just as people learn to draw and paint by copying the masters." If you are writing to a specific genre audience, you need to know what that audience expects. Deconstructing and analyzing top authors in the genre you want to write in is the best thing you can do. And read, read, read.

MIND YOUR YESSES AND NOS

Lots of little words mess us writers up. Here's a list of some with their proper spelling (and note that these are lowercased in a sentence).

- yesses and nos and maybes
- dos and don'ts
- ifs, ands, and buts
- I sent thank-yous
- coworker (used to be hyphenated but now it's not)
- How many "to be continueds" should we expect? (put the s inside the quotes if you are pluralizing a word or expression)
- Mind your p's and q's
- Dot your i's and cross your t's
- abc's

However, letters used for grades are to be capitalized:

- He got all A's on his report card, and she got two B's.

If you mind your p's and q's, I'll be happy to give you all A's on your behavior report card!

TIP FOR FICTION WRITERS: When writing fast-action scenes, you want the reader to read fast and feel the story is speeding up. To help do this, trim down sentences to make them as short as possible, leaving only the most essential words. Keep paragraphs short—two to three lines at most, wherever you can. You can pare down even more by replacing long words with shorter ones. Think about using incomplete sentences, or even single-word sentences.

BEING FORWARD ABOUT FOREWORDS

It really shouldn't be too hard to keep these words straight, but I see them misspelled all the time. Many writers put a "forward" in their book. And at the end, they have an "afterward." Yes, they might be acting a bit *forward* when they introduce their story, and maybe *afterward*, they have something to say. But *afterward* is an adverb (it modifies a verb), and *forward* can be either an adverb or an adjective—and even a verb. Okay, there is a noun form of *forward*, as you football players might be wont to point out. But the key to this mystery is tied up in four little letters, which form the word *word*.

What does *fore* mean (and I don't mean what you yell out when you hit the golf ball)? It basically means "before." So if you are going to put a bunch of words *before* the body of your book, those will be forewords. Hence, the correct term *foreword*. Do I really need to go through this explanation for *afterword*? I think not.

Well, then, is there a difference between foreword/afterword and prologue/epilogue? Good question (and you can spell those last two words without the "ue" as a variation—same with dialog). Usually a foreword is written by someone other than the author of the book. Or it might be better to say that if someone else writes an introduction or commentary at the front of a book, it would not be called a prologue. A foreword

usually contains prefatory comments. A prologue, in contrast, is often assumed to be material related and connected to the rest of the book, not something ancillary. Same goes for the afterword and epilogue.

A note about epilogues in novels: I see many final chapters called epilogues that are really just the last chapters of a novel wrapping up the story. An epilogue basically summarizes and reflects on the story as a whole. It isn't the "ending" of the novel's plot. A true epilogue will feel different from the rest of the novel, and may be presented as if years later, with a character reflecting back on the whole story or telling how things turned out for all the players. The kind of thing we see often in plays, where a character sums everything up (think *The Tempest* or *A Midsummer Night's Dream*).

So, good night unto you all. Give me your hands, if we be friends, And Robin shall restore amends. Amen.

NOTES

NOTES

PUNCTUATION

COMMAS, ETC.

Personally, I really dislike the use of *etc., et al, i.e.,* and *e.g.* Think about it—
how many people really know what *i.e.* stands for—or even care? Why
would we in this day and age use weird abbreviations of Latin terms that
we as a culture have long forgotten? If you are like me, you probably forget
whether to use i.e. or e.g. in certain instances.

"In other words" and "for example" seem to be a lot easier to understand
and don't sound so hoity-toity to me. But if you really have a hankering to
use *etc.* (*etcetera* literally means "and others of the same kind"), it is
preceded and followed by a comma when it is the final item in a series
(unless it ends a sentence). Such equivalents as *and so forth* and *and the like*
are usually treated the same way. (In formal prose, *etc.* should be avoided,
though it is usually acceptable in lists and tables, in notes, and within
parentheses.)

- I bought my school supplies (pencils, notebook paper, etc., that the
  teacher told us to buy) this evening.
- The ingredients I needed, such as flour, sugar, salt, etc., were in short
  supply at the market.
- My favorite movies, like *Star Wars, Evolution, Galaxy Quest,* and the
  like, were all checked out at the movie store.

But think about rewriting, reworking, revising, etc., if you are going to use
a lot of old-fashioned abbreviations! Your writing will be a whole lot more
interesting. Oh, and if you're using an ampersand—&—don't use a comma:
"I work at the law firm Tom, Dick & Harry."

TIP FOR FICTION WRITERS: ""I am always chilled and astonished
by the would-be writers who ask me for advice and admit, quite
blithely, that they 'don't have time to read.' This is like a guy
starting up Mount Everest saying that he didn't have time to buy
any rope or pitons." ~ Stephen King

I Wonder, Where Is That Comma?

This is a comma rule that I wasn't even sure of myself and had to look up! I've seen it handled many different ways in manuscripts, but here's what *Chicago Manual of Style* says:

> Questions are sometimes included within another sentence either directly or indirectly—not as a quotation but as part of the sentence as a whole. A direct question (unless it comes at the beginning of a sentence) is usually introduced by a comma. A direct question may take an initial capital letter if it is relatively long or has internal punctuation.

Here are some examples:

- Suddenly he asked himself, where am I headed?
- The question on everyone's mind was, how are we going to tell her?
- Legislators had to be asking themselves, Can the fund be used for the current emergency, or must it remain dedicated to its original purpose?

If the result seems awkward, rephrase as an indirect question. An indirect question does not require a question mark, nor does it need to be set off with a comma. Indirect questions are never capitalized (except at the beginning of a sentence). Here are ways to rephrase:

- Suddenly he asked himself where he was headed.
- The question of how to tell her was on everyone's mind.
- Ursula wondered why her watch had stopped ticking.
- Where to find a reliable clock is the question of the hour.

And don't put a question mark at the end of these sentences just because the word *question* is in there or a question is implied. I'm amazed at how many sentences I come across that are not questions but have question marks at the end!

USING COMMAS, SINCE THEY'RE NEEDED

Meaning is everything, and that little comma can really make a big difference in your meaning. I especially pay attention to phrases that have *because* and *since* in them. See if you can tell the difference in meaning with each pair of sentences:

- I didn't go to the store because you were angry.
- I didn't go to the store, because you were angry.

In the first instance, my going to the store had nothing to do with your anger, and that's what I'm telling you. But with the comma, the sentence means "I didn't go to the store for the reason that you were angry." Your anger kept me from going to the store, which is the opposite of the first sentence's meaning.

- I played football since I was nine.
- I played football, since I was nine.

The word *since* has some different meanings, so by using the comma, you're being clear. In the first sentence, I started playing football at age nine. (It would be clearer to write "I've been playing football since I was nine.") The second sentence gives the reason I played football—because I was nine, implying I was at a qualifiable age. So, to quote my eighth-grade English teacher, Mr. Holtby: "Say what you mean. Don't say what you don't mean."

> *TIP FOR FICTION WRITERS:* In fiction, there may be places where you want to fudge the comma rules to achieve a certain effect. For example, if you have a character speaking excitedly with run-on sentences, you may choose to leave the commas out to give her words a hurried, frenetic feel. With speech, you want the character's personality and voice to come through, so comma accuracy should be weighed alongside these elements in your novel.

COMMAS THAT ARE, INDEED, USEFUL

Commas—sometimes paired with semicolons—are traditionally used to set off adverbs, such as *however, therefore,* and *indeed.* When the adverb is essential to the meaning of the clause, or if no pause is intended or desired, commas are not needed.

- A truly efficient gasoline-powered engine remains, however, a pipe dream.
- Indeed, not one test subject accurately predicted the amount of soup in the bowl.
- Compare to:
- If you cheat and are therefore disqualified, you may also risk losing your scholarship.
- That was indeed the outcome of the study.

If you, also, use the word *also* or *too,* you, too, should offset those words in the middle of a sentence. Just FYI, *Chicago* style prefers not using a comma with *too* at the end of a sentence. I like that rule too. (I just gave examples of all these rules in these sentences, in case you might have missed them.)

TIP FOR FICTION WRITERS: Flannery O'Connor wrote: "I'm a full-time believer in writing habits . . . You may be able to do without them if you have genius, but most of us only have talent and this is simply something that has tobe assisted all the time by physical and mental habits or it dries up and blows away. . . . Of course you have to make your habits in this conform to what you can do. I write only about two hours every day because that's all the energy I have, but I don't let anything interfere with those two hours, at the same time and the same place." Make writing a daily habit.

THEY TRAVEL IN PAIRS . . . SOMETIMES

Often there are subtle differences in the choice of whether or not to use a comma. Whenever a comma is used to set off an element (such as "1928" or "Minnesota" in the first two examples below), a second comma is required if the phrase or sentence continues (completing the thought) beyond the element being set off.

- June 5, 1928, lives on in the memories of only a handful of us.
- Sledding in Duluth, Minnesota, is made fun by that city's hills and frigid winters.

I often see sentences that set off a phrase in the middle but only use one comma. It's best to check and see if you really need a pair. If you are inserting a phrase that can be removed and leaves a complete sentence with an unchanged meaning, you do need a pair of commas. These are called "parenthetical elements" that serve as an explanation or comment.

Wrong:

- When I went to the store, at the request of my mother I bought a gallon of milk.
- Sometimes, when the sun is out I go for an early run.
- He ate a huge, almost gigantic sandwich.
- Correct:
- When I went to the store, at the request of my mother, I bought a gallon of milk.
- Sometimes, when the sun is out, I go for an early run.
- He ate a huge, almost gigantic, sandwich.
- You bought a gallon of milk whether or not the person you are talking to knows your mom sent you. Or you can write this:
- "When I went to the store at the request of my mother, I bought a gallon of milk."

This is also correct, but you need to be aware of the difference in emphasis. If you offset the phrase with two commas, you are implying the phrase offset is not essential information. With this new example of one comma, you are including the information about the mother's request as important.

You can also leave out both commas and write: "Sometimes when the sun is out, I go for an early run." Offsetting "when the sun is out" makes it essential to the sentence, implying that you go for a run *because* the sun is out. It's all about subtle emphasis and importance.

COMMA GET A HANDLE ON COMMAS

Those dreaded commas. I think commas cause more confusion than any other bit of punctuation. Writers either overuse them or don't use them enough or properly. So I've created numerous entries on comma rules to help you get a handle on those slippery things.

Material quoted in the form of dialog or from text is traditionally introduced with a comma. If a quotation is introduced by *that, whether,* or a similar conjunction, no comma is needed. If a quoted phrase completes a thought started in the sentence, you don't need the comma.

These are correctly written:

- It was Thoreau who wrote, "One generation abandons the enterprises of another like stranded vessels."
- She replied, "I hope you aren't referring to us."
- Was it your mother who used to say that "a penny saved is a penny earned"?
- You are now wondering whether "to speak now or forever hold your peace."

Someone once said, "Commas are the bane of an author's existence," but I don't know who said that.

TIP FOR FICTION WRITERS: **Many writers forget that not all characters know what the writer knows or would use the same words she'd use. Poor word choices stand out when characters use words they should be unfamiliar with or words that require specific knowledge they couldn't have. Writers sometimes remember to use the correct words for character dialog and yet forget when they write character thoughts. Incorrect word use by characters is obvious and may have readers thinking about the mechanics and foundations of the book rather than the story, which is not what you want to have happen.**

SERIAL COMMAS ARE SERIOUS STUFF

Serial commas are commas that separate items in a series and in particular pertain to the use of a comma with the last item listed. Many people ignore this rule, and I'm pretty sure it's standard policy (to ignore) this rule in AP (article writing) style. Which doesn't make sense to me.

It's very important to always use a serial comma.

The example often used to show the need for the serial comma is this line: "I'd like to thank my parents, God and Mother Teresa, for inspiring me."

Well, by not using the serial comma between *God* and *Mother Teresa*, you can see how the meaning of this sentence gets really wacky. I mean, who in their right mind would claim their parents are God and Mother Teresa?

The way to punctuate this correctly so as to avoid such a weird interpretation is "I'd like to thank my parents, God, and Mother Teresa for inspiring me."

Entire books have been written on this topic (see *Eats, Shoots & Leaves: The Zero Tolerance Approach to Punctuation* for a great book that stresses the need to be careful with those tiny bits of punctuation).

So, whenever you have a list, be sure you use a comma after each item in that list. You don't necessarily need one after the very last item—that depends upon the phrase to follow, but we won't get into that in this entry.

TIP FOR FICTION WRITERS: **Cutting lines, paragraphs, and even whole scenes is a vital and powerful skill for writers to develop. A writer needs to look at each section and ask, "Do I need this?" Overly wordy sentences, extended paragraphs, and repetition should all be removed. Any section that fails to move the plot forward should be cut. Cutting back the work is painful, but if done correctly will improve your book tenfold.**

SEMICOLONS: COMMONLY MISUSED BITS OF PUNCTUATION

The semicolon is the most commonly misused punctuation mark. Bryan Garner (*Garner's Modern American Usage*) calls the semicolon a "supercomma" because it's more than a comma. If you can remember these uses for a semicolon, you will be a super semicolon user.

Use a semicolon to separate two independent clauses that are not joined by one of these conjunctions: *for, and, nor, but, or, yet, so* (think of *fanboys* as an acronym to remember them all). For example:

- John was the first to cross the finish line; Bob couldn't find it.
- Using one of the conjunctions, the sentence would require a comma:
- John was the first to cross the finish line, but Bob couldn't find it.
- When adverbs like however, therefore, indeed, besides, or nevertheless are used to join two independent clauses, use a semicolon before the adverb.
- Bob ran five miles every day; nevertheless, he couldn't keep up with John.

Use a semicolon to separate items in a list when the items are already separated by commas.

- The winners of the marathon hailed from Little Rock, Arkansas; Denver, Colorado; and Kodiak Island, Alaska.

Be careful not to confuse a semicolon with a colon. They perform two different functions. The semicolon invites the reader to pause; the colon moves the reader forward. The colon precedes a series of elements that amplify or expand on what comes before the colon. Also make sure to use a colon only after a complete sentence, not a fragment. For example:

- Incorrect: My favorite weekend activities include: sleeping in, pigging out, and cheering for the home team.
- Correct: I'm looking forward to my weekend activities: sleeping in, pigging out, and cheering for the home team.

On another note, fiction writers often misuse semicolons. The most common misuse is in setting apart a phrase, and what should be used here is an em dash, such as in this example:

- Incorrect: He lost his money at the slot machines; every single penny.
- Correct: He lost his money at the slot machines—every single penny.

So, try hard not to misuse this tiny bit of punctuation.

MAKE A DASH FOR IT

If you're not familiar with printers' terminology, you may not know the term *em dash*. But as a writer and reader, you're no doubt familiar with its use. Strunk and White describe the dash as a "mark of separation stronger than a comma, less formal than a colon, and more relaxed than parentheses."

It helps to distinguish it from its shorter cousin, the *en dash*, if you know that it draws its name from the typesetting world. The em dash is the width of a capital letter *M*, while the en dash is the width of the *N*. So as not to overwhelm you, let's just look at the usage for the em dash and save the shorter dash for another entry.

An em dash signals a sudden change in thought or sets off an element that explains or amplifies. It can function as an alternative to parentheses, which some readers may find more distracting than a dash, commas, or a colon.

Note: In a lot of the manuscripts I edit and critique, I notice the use of a semicolon in place of the required dash. I think writers choose that bit of punctuation because they don't know what else to use. But the em dash is almost always what they need in those places.

- He told them not to be afraid—just to mind their own business (a comma doesn't quite offset the phrase enough).
- That night—the night of Mr. Liddle's return—was no different from the others (alternative to parentheses—less visually disruptive. Whenever you interrupt a sentence like this, you want to use a pair of em dashes).
- The rear axle began to make a noise—a grinding, chattering, teeth-gritting rasp (alternative to a colon).

Am em dash is also used in dialog to indicate a break, interruption, or hesitation in the conversation:

- "I'm sorry, Heather. I can hear the ice in the—"
- "And you assume I'm drinking—?"

Notice, there's no end punctuation (other than the quotation mark) after the em dash.

Like all punctuation marks, use the dash judiciously. Bryan Garner maintains that the em dash may be the most under-used punctuation mark in American writing. It can bring clarity to a sentence clogged with commas or bring just the right visual punch to convey the author's intent. I happen to love them and—without a doubt—use them a lot! And there you have the long and short of dashes.

WHAT ARE THOSE LONG HYPHENS ALL ABOUT?

Sorting out the family of dashes—hyphens, en dashes, and em dashes—can give writers a headache. Before I started studying copyediting, I had no idea there were things called *en dashes*. I just thought they were long hyphens and caused by the font I was looking at. Silly me.

I then discovered this odd little bit of punctuation that pretty much every writer ignores. So why should you care? Don't get me started on that. Writers should learn when to use each bit of punctuation—if only to spare their copyeditor time and effort (and to score brownie points!).

The hyphen is the shortest member of the family. I would guess that everyone knows what a hyphen is and (mostly) how to use one. We use hyphens in compound words—to connect numbers that are not inclusive, such as telephone numbers, social security numbers, or ISBN numbers—and to break a word at the end of a line. Your word processor is automatically going to do this if you choose that option in your default settings.

The en dash is a little wider than a hyphen, although sometimes it's hard to spot. It is used primarily to indicate a range of numbers involving dates, times, and page numbers; occasionally it connects words. It signifies *up to and including* or *through*.

- Girls Scouts is for girls who are 9–12 years of age.
- Hurricane season runs from June 1–November 30 in the tropics.
- Read pages 97–150 for tomorrow's assignment.
- In these examples, you would not use an en dash:
- I bought the July-September issue of Great Grammar. (This is not a range of inclusive items. It implies from July through September. See the next example.)
- From 25-50 people showed up. (Don't use an en dash with numbers that follow the words from or between.)
- When an en dash is used to show a game score or directions, it signifies to.
- Boston won the World Series 6–5.
- The prevailing winds in the plains are west–east.

An en dash can also be used in an open-ended date range, such as the dates of a living person or a serial publication. In none of these instances should a space be inserted between the dash and the text—either before or after. (Tip: Alt + Hyphen on the number pad will make an en dash.)

HYPHENATION—NOT-SO-EASY-TO-UNDERSTAND RULES

I think the most errors I see when editing manuscripts have to do with hyphenation.

There are so many rules, and sometimes no consistency to them. The best advice I can give you is to get a CD of *Merriam-Webster's Collegiate Dictionary, 11th Edition,* and download it onto your computer. I use it all the time, every day, as it is the accepted authority in book publishing. (Note: The CD is included in the print book in the back, so this way you will have the book as a reference too.)

The Chicago Manual of Style takes precedence over *M-W*, though, so if you don't have the *CMOS 16th Edition,* you should buy it. However, it's a very expensive and huge tome, so I highly encourage you to subscribe to the online version so you can access it anywhere you are. Refer to it whenever you are unsure whether a word should be hyphenated or not.

Often *CMOS* will refer you to check *M-W* for their take on a particular word, so you need both tools. With both of these resources at your fingertips, you will be able to go through your book and clean it up. Remember—your spell-checker will steer you wrong a lot! It will often tag some words as not being in the dictionary when they are correct, and it will sometimes let a misspelling slip through, so use your spell-checker judiciously!

Many hyphenation rules deal with modifying a noun (putting an adjective or compound adjective before the noun), as shown in some examples below.

Here are some basic and common usages of hyphenated style:

- My sixteen-year-old is taking ballet classes from a seventy-year-old woman.
- He's wearing a dark-green coat and a blue-gray sweater. [But you would say, "His coat is dark green."]
- It's a black-and-white photo. [But you would say, "The truth is black and white."]
- I'm taking a fiction-writing workshop.
- This is cutting-edge technology. [But you would say, "This tech is cutting edge."]
- I'm working a twelve-hour-a-day schedule. [But you would say, "I'm working a twelve-hour day."]
- This book is a nineteenth-century romance with twenty-first-century dialog.

A lot of words we tend to hyphenate should be one closed-up word, so check both the handy hyphenation chart and *Merriam-Webster's Collegiate Dictionary, 11th Edition.*

PREFIXES THAT PUT YOU IN A FIX WITH HYPHENATION

Hyphenation is the bane of many a writer. Wilson Follett, author of *Modern American Usage: A Guide*, wrote, "Nothing gives away the incompetent amateur more quickly than the typescript that neglects this mark of punctuation or that employs it where it is not wanted."

For hyphenation rules, the best advice I can give you is to consult the CMOS hyphenation chart (you can Google it and print it out!) and *Merriam-Webster's Collegiate Dictionary*. But I'll try to cover some basics to help get you familiar with the most common hyphenation issues.

When considering hyphenation, here are your options:

- Open (two words, no hyphenation)
- Closed (one word)
- Hyphenated (connecting two words with a hyphen)

Let's take a look at prefixes. British English is more likely to use the hyphen than American English. Most compounds formed with prefixes are closed in AmE, whether they are nouns, verb, adjectives, or adverbs. But here are some exceptions. These constructions require a hyphen following the prefix:

- Before a capitalized word or a numeral, such as post-Roman or mid-August
- Before a compound term, such as non-self-disclosure
- To separate double vowels, such as anti-intellectual or co-organizers (many "co" words are closed up though, so check your dictionary)
- When a prefix or combining form stands alone, such as over- and underused, macro- and microeconomics
- Here are a couple of prefixes that are quite consistent in their open, closed, or hyphenated forms:
- all – most adjective compounds are hyphenated, while most adverb compounds are not.
  - ➤ Adjectives: all-inclusive, all-around, all-powerful
  - ➤ Adverbs: all over, all out, all along
- cross – most compounds formed with cross are hyphenated; a few are closed.
  - ➤ cross-country, cross-checking, crossbar, crosspiece, crosswalk

Many of us tend to hyphenate words with prefixes, but much of the time we should close these words up. That includes words that begin with *anti, co, counter, extra, hyper, inter,* and many more. So, best to look them up first in the dictionary, and if you can't find the word as one combined word, then hyphenate it.

MORE HANDY HYPHENATION RULES

It's a good thing to know that in some cases the meaning of a word changes if you hyphenate it. Take a look at these pairs of words:

- rebound: to spring back or recover; re-bound: tied again (retied)
- recollect: remember; re-collect: collect again (regather)
- recover: heal, restore; re-cover: to cover something again
- recreate: to engage in recreation; re-create: to create again

Notice that this is an issue with words that begin with the prefix *re*.

The prefix *self* has interesting rules. Most adjectives with this prefix are hyphenated, except when the prefix *un* is applied or *self* is followed by a suffix (if you've forgotten, a suffix is the opposite of a prefix; it's an affix at the end of a word). Examples:

- Self-effacing, self-conscious, self-sustaining, unselfconscious, selfless, selfish
- Here are some correctly written words I often see hyphenated erroneously in manuscripts:
- stepbrother, stepmother (But you would write step-granddaughter.)
- toothache, stomachache (*Ache* as a prefix is always a closed word.)
- halfway, halfhearted, wholehearted (Check your dictionary for words with *half*.)
- catlike, Christlike, doglike, horselike (If the word is not in the dictionary, or if *like* is added on to a proper name, hyphenate it.)
- ongoing, online (Some *on* words are often hyphenated.)
- 5 percent, a 10 percent solution (Note that both the noun and adjective forms are open.)
- nonnegotiable, nonviolent, nonaddictive (Words with *non* are almost always closed.)
- cofounder, codirector, copublisher, coordinator, codependent (Same with *co*.)

As you can see, there is no easy blanket rule for hyphenation as it pertains to prefixes, so always check your dictionary. (Be sure to use Merriam-Webster's Collegiate 11th Edition, as that is the accepted authority. Other dictionaries may not follow the same rules.)

A SIMPLE HYPHENATION RULE THAT IS WELL ADVISED

One hyphenation rule that you can almost take to the bank is this one: When you use a compound adjective (or phrasal adjective) before a noun, use a hyphen. When the phrasal adjective comes after the noun, it is usually open.

See how this plays out with various parts of speech:

- Middle-class neighborhood, but the neighborhood is middle class (adjective + noun)
- Open-ended question, but the question was open ended (adjective + participle)
- Much-needed rain, but rain was much needed (adverb + participle or adjective)

But adverbs ending in *ly* + participle or adjective are open whether they are used before or after a noun.

- Overly protective mother
- Highly skilled employees

Likewise, compounds with more, most, less, least, and very are usually open unless the meaning could be confused.

- Most literate employees (referring to number of employees)
- Most-literate employees (referring to literacy capacity)
- Flag-waving citizen, but citizens waving flags (noun + participle)
- Cutting-edge technology, but technology is cutting edge. (participle + noun)
- Participle + *up*, *out*, and similar adverbs:
- Fired-up employees, but employees were fired up.
- Tuckered-out children, but children were tuckered out.

You can see there is a general rule here. When you place the compound *after* a noun, you usually leave it in open construction. When it comes *before* the noun, it's usually closed.

But always double check the word in your dictionary to make sure it's not one of those exceptions to the rule, which is a common occurrence in the English language.

HYPHENATING NUMBERS AND COLORS

The same hyphenation rule that applies to compound modifiers and the various parts of speech also applies to various categories of words, such as time, color, numbers, and age. Hyphenate the compound when it appears before the noun—no hyphen following the noun.

- Age: "a three-year-old girl," but "she was three years old"
- Colors: "a blue-green plate," but "the dish was blue green"
- Numbers: "He was twenty-five," but "my grandfather lived to one hundred five."
- A number paired with a noun will be hyphenated before the noun it modifies, but open after.
- "a first-year student," but "this student is in his first year"
- "a 917-page volume," but "a volume with 917 pages"
- Note the use of two hyphens when a range or interval is indicated:
- It would be a ten- to thirty-minute wait for a seat, the hostess advised.

Ten and *thirty* both modify *wait*; there is no need to write "ten-minute to thirty-minute wait," but it is necessary to connect the phrase with the first hyphen to show that these elements are equal and belong together.

Ordinal numbers follow the hyphen-before, open-after rule.

- "First floor," but "first-floor apartment"
- "Third place," but "third-place ribbon"
- "Thirty-third row," but "thirty-third-row seats"

And pairing up an ordinal number and superlative follows the same rule.

- "First place," but "first-place finish"
- "Second-to-last place," but "finished second to last"

And then there are fractions. When the fraction is used as a noun, leave it open; when it is an adjective, hyphenate it.

- "Half hour," but "half-hour lesson"
- "Quarter mile," but "a quarter-mile run"

Fractions, such as one-half, two-thirds, and three-quarters, are hyphenated.

I hope you had a front-row lesson for this ten-minute discussion.

WHEN YOU DON'T WANT TO HYPHENATE

Writers often hyphenate when they aren't supposed to. It always seems to make sense that if you have two words that sound like they're connected, you should stick a hyphen between them. But not so. Here are some word combinations that are usually open:

Proper nouns and adjectives relating to geography or nationality, unless the first term is a prefix:

- Chinese Americans, North Central region, African American, African American president

But you would write:

- US-Mexico border, Spanish-American organizations

Chemical terms:

- sodium chloride, sodium chloride solution

Foreign phrases—open unless hyphenated in the original language. Foreign phrases and words are also italicized:

- *A priori, in vitro* fertilization, but *vis-à-vis* for clarity and meaning. (The actual meaning is face-to-face, also hyphenated.)

Numbers and abbreviations:

- 25 mi. trip, 3 oz. cup, 5K race

Numbers and percentages:

- 75 percent, 4.6 percent

Noun and numeral or enumerator:

- Type 2 diabetes, size 12 font, page 1 placement

So if you're writing a popular paranormal novel, you might be writing about an American Martian undead vampire zombie. No hyphens needed!

WHAT ABOUT THOSE TECHY TERMS?

I would be remiss if I didn't spend a moment going over hyphenation as it applies to technology-related words. This is an area of our vocabulary that grows right along with our expanding technological world. Language is always changing, but technology words present a special challenge to the writer. I feel it's mostly because many grammar guides that are written for the tech industry have rules that conflict with *The Chicago Manual of Style*.

Technological words are coined by folks who are more interested in technology than grammar. Many are programmers who are confined by requirements that demand the use of a single string of characters. That explains why these types of compound words begin their vocabulary life as closed terms and are most likely to be adopted that way for general use.

Here again, context is critical.

- Scientific or technical publications are more likely to use the closed form, for example: *screensaver, fileserver,* and *screenshot.*
- General-purpose publications will render them open: *screen saver, file server, screen shot.*

Here are the current guidelines for a few frequently used technology terms:

- *Electronic* is shortened to *e-* to identify anything and everything transmitted digitally or electronically, so *e-mail, e-book, e-commerce* are all hyphenated. But when a proper noun follows the prefix, there's no hyphen, such as *eBay.*

The best example of the progression of a word from introduction to mainstream usage is *website.* It has evolved from the capitalized open rendering (*Web site*) to the current, almost universally accepted lowercase, closed version: *website.* Some journalistic publications may retain the older variation.

CMOS recognizes *web* as a generic term when used alone or in combination with other words. Thus *webcam, webcast, webmaster* are acceptable, but the compound adjective *web-related* is hyphenated.

Where would we be without Wi-Fi? We all know it as the technology that enables us to connect to the Internet wherever we are, but exactly what it stands for and how to render it is up for debate. This seems to be one of those words in transition. Look for a definitive rendering once it's actually accepted as part of the general vernacular. For now, you may see *Wi-Fi, wifi,* or *WiFi.* Check the style guide for the publication or publisher you're writing for, if applicable.

ARE YOU ASKING A QUESTION OR NOT?

Wondering when to use a question mark? The answer is simple. When you expect an answer. Yet, I continually see writers getting "question mark happy" and sticking these bits of punctuation where they have no business being.

Direct questions—the kind journalists ask to get a story—demand an answer. They are often referred to as the 5 (or 6) *W*'s: who, what, when, where, why, and how.

What happened? Who was involved? When did it happen? Where? Why? How?

Direct questions almost always begin with some variation of the 5 *W*'s. If one of these isn't the first word in the sentence, it's probably in there some place, like: "Well, just *what* are you doing in there?" or "Just *who* do you think you are?" And then there are sentences that begin with *could, should,* or *would*. It shouldn't be hard to tell when a sentence is a question, should it?

Sentences that begin with a being verb like *are, is, were,* and the like also indicate a direction question.

- Are you going to Scarborough Fair?
- Is anyone going with you?
- May I come along?

All these questions demand an answer and a question mark.

And now to complicate things, just a little. We also pose indirect questions, but we don't expect answers to these questions.

- I wondered why he went in there.
- I asked her what the problem was.

Sometimes writers prefer not to have question marks following rhetorical questions (a matter of choice):

- Who could blame him.

No one really expects an answer to a question like that. And neither do these indirect questions require question marks.

Got it?

STAY INSIDE THE QUOTE MARKS

Unless you are writing British (UK) style, always put commas and periods within the quotation marks in speech. I'm not sure why so many writers don't follow this simple rule, and I often see them using single quotes randomly instead of double quotes. The rule is that you use double quotes for everything, unless you are putting a quote (single quote) inside another quote (double quote).

Wrong:

- "Here's your newspaper", he said.
- He called her a "wacko".
- They call him a 'nutcase.'

Correct:

- "Here's your newspaper," he said.
- He called her a "wacko."
- They call him a "nutcase."

The exceptions are em dashes . . .

- "I wouldn't do that"—he gave her a stern look—"if I were you!"
- . . . and semicolons, if used in this type of manner:
- I think you're "cute"; however, not first thing in the morning.
- There are also occasions when question marks belong between single and double quotes, such as:
- "What do you mean by 'I'm dumb'?"

The context determines the placement of question marks (and exclamation marks).

TIP FOR FICTION WRITERS: **Give it a rest. If time allows, set your writing aside for a few hours (or days) after you've finished for the day or reached a goal, then proofread it with fresh eyes. You're more likely to see what you've actually written than what you thought you wrote.**

SCARE QUOTES ARE NOT ALL THAT SCARY

There's a time and place for every punctuation mark. Using any of them excessively or incorrectly is, well, just plain scary. In fact, there's a style for punctuating a word or phrase that you are using in a nontraditional way: scare quotes.

Occasionally you will use a word in a nonstandard way. You may want to note that you're using it as slang or to convey irony or sarcasm. Setting the word off in quotation marks tells the reader "I know this isn't the way you normally understand this word." Or "This is not a term I came up with."

For example:

- The commissioner's platform of infrastructure "investment" didn't fool astute voters; he lost by ten percentage points. (The writer uses *investment* as a euphemism for tax increase.)
- Joe and his "harem" showed up at the game just in time for the tip-off. (*Harem* is used as slang or irony here, not in the traditional meaning of the word.)

Scare quotes are very useful in making clear your "different" meaning. We sometimes mimic these written quotes when speaking by making quote marks with our fingers, to imply the same thing.

Once you've alerted readers that you're using the term as slang, euphemism, or another nontraditional usage, there's no need to continue setting it off with quotation marks if you need to keep referring to that word or term. Readers are pretty smart; they will get it. Continuing to use the quotation marks will be scary. Trust me.

TIP FOR FICTION WRITERS: Some writers go by their "ear" when it comes to punctuation. They use commas and semicolons to increase or slow the pace and rhythm of their prose. Some base their decisions on how a sentence looks on the page, perhaps not wanting to clutter with unnecessary commas. But the best approach is to stick closely to the rules of punctuation to ensure your sentences will be read correctly, and to avoid complaint that your work has not been edited correctly.

DON'T ABUSE THE DOT, DOT, DOTS

Writers often succumb to dot abuse. Well, I've heard some people call ellipses "dots." I'm not talking about the candy here. These are very useful bits of punctuation that every writer will need to use sometime. But these three little dots get tossed around too much and are used where they shouldn't.

The ellipsis consists of three evenly spaced dots (periods) with spaces between the ellipsis and surrounding letters or other marks. The only time you don't leave a space between an ellipsis "dot" and a surrounding mark is when it falls next to a quotation mark:

- "... I ... I can't breathe ..."

Notice that it is perfectly correct to include punctuation in speech alongside ellipses as desired:

- "Am I ... going to die ... ?"
- "But I have to get there before ... ," he said.

Ellipses have a few different functions. Here are the main uses for an ellipsis:

- To indicate trailing, faltering, or interrupted speech (which is the most common use for fiction writers)
- To indicate text that is missing or omitted from a quotation (there are specific style formats for that)

Like exclamation marks or italics, one can overdo the use of ellipses. I sometimes see ellipsis abuse all over the place. Ellipses used for sudden cutoff of speech (that's where you use an em dash, not an ellipsis), for pauses when there should be none, or for a poetic feel (really doesn't work). Ellipses running amok when they should be used sparingly and appropriately.

Just so you know: If you are quoting material and omit words following the end of a sentence, you'll want to use four dots (one is the period for that sentence) like this:

- "Six people were injured. ... whether any survived is unknown at this time."

Another good use of ellipses (although this is not a rule but a handy style choice) is when you are showing only one side of a phone conversation, and you want to indicate those pauses showing the character is listening:

- "Yes? ... This is he ... No, I don't want to buy a vacuum ... no, not an encyclopedia either. Good-bye."

By the way, those "dots" are called ellipsis points or ellipsis marks. But you can call them "dot, dot, dots," if that makes you happy!

NOTES

NOTES

CAPITALIZATION

POINT ME IN THE RIGHT DIRECTION

Okay, maybe you're ready for some tricky rules about capitalization regarding geographic regions. If not, swallow hard and take a look. Many writers have trouble knowing when to capitalize a geographical region, and there is no easy rule. Here are a few examples showing the correct way to capitalize:

- the Great Plains; the northern plains; the plains (but Plains Indians)
- the Midwest, midwestern, a midwesterner (as of the United States)
- the North, northern, a northerner (of a country); the North, Northern, Northerner (in American Civil War contexts); Northern California; North Africa, North African countries, in northern Africa; North America, North American, the North American continent; the North Atlantic, a northern Atlantic route; the Northern Hemisphere; the Far North; north, northern, northward, to the north (directions)
- the Northeast, the Northwest, northwestern, northeastern, a northwesterner, a northeasterner (as of the United States); the Pacific Northwest; the Northwest Passage
- the poles; the North Pole; the North Polar ice cap; the South Pole; polar regions; Antarctica; the Arctic
- the South, southern, a southerner (of a country); the South, Southern, a Southerner (in American Civil War contexts); the Deep South; Southern California; the South of France (region); Southeast Asia; South Africa, South African (referring to the Republic of South Africa); southern Africa (referring to the southern part of the continent); south, southern, southward, to the south (directions)
- the Southeast, the Southwest, southeastern, southwestern, a southeasterner, a southwesterner (as of the United States)

As I've mentioned before, the tendency is to *lowercase unless the name or phrase is referring to something akin to a proper name or title*. But when it comes to specific regions of the world, some are considered "worthy" of capitalization while others aren't.

We in California were happy to see *Chicago* add Northern California to its list of worthies in the 16th edition. Why it wasn't seen on the same level as Southern California all these years, I guess we may never know. And I hope you noticed the absence of hyphens in those compound terms, like *southwesterner*. Even my WordPress spell-check gives me every possible option except the correct one (which should give you a clue as to how correct those spell-checkers are)!

DON'T GET CAPPY HAPPY

Writers seem to get "cappy" happy (yes, I just made up that term). I often see the most random terms and phrases capitalized, but generally the rule is that *if it's not a specific proper name of something, it doesn't need to have the first letter capitalized.* Here are just a few types of words that often erroneously get capitalized. All the terms and phrases listed below are correct.

Student status:

- freshman or first-year student
- sophomore

Academic degrees:

- a master's degree
- a doctorate; a fellowship
- master of business administration (MBA)

Ethnic groups (common designations) unless a particular publisher or author prefers otherwise:

- black people; blacks; people of color
- white people; whites

Terms denoting socioeconomic classes:

- the middle class; a middle-class neighborhood
- the upper-middle class; an upper-middle-class family
- blue-collar workers
- the aristocracy
- homeless people

Terms denoting generations:

- the me generation
- baby boomer(s)
- generation X; generation Y; generation Z
- the MTV generation

Note that when referring to an academic department, you do use initial caps, but do not capitalize *the*: "I went to the Department of Natural History yesterday to speak to the dean."

PLACES TO CALL TO YOUR ATTENTION

Popular names of places, or epithets, are usually capitalized. Quotation marks are not needed. Note that where the article *the* is used, it is not capitalized.

- the Fertile Crescent
- the Gaza Strip
- the Gulf
- the Holy City
- the Jewish Quarter
- the Lake District
- the Left Bank
- the Promised Land
- Silicon Valley
- Skid Row

Names of mountains, rivers, oceans, islands, and so forth are capitalized. The generic term (mountain, for example) is also capitalized when used as part of the name.

- the Bering Strait
- the Mediterranean Sea; the Mediterranean
- the Pacific Ocean; the Pacific and the Atlantic Oceans
- the Great Barrier Reef
- the Hawaiian Islands; Hawaii; but the island of Hawaii
- Mount Washington; Mount Rainier; Mounts Washington and Rainier
- the Rocky Mountains; the Rockies
- Death Valley
- the Continental Divide

The best and simplest way to generalize capitalization rules is to consider whether what you are writing is a proper name or something more general. Proper names should have initial caps. General terms do not. That's not always the case, but when in doubt, default to that principle.

CAPITALIZE ON THESE TIPS ON CAPITALIZATION

Most writers get confused about capitalization. There are a lot of diverse rules, but here are some easy ones you can learn.

Capitalize compass directions when they refer to identifiable places like the American West but not general directions, like "Go west, young man."

- I'm heading out west.
- I'm going to live in the West.

Capitalize historical eras:

- the Roaring Twenties
- the Ice Age
- the Cold War
- the Great Depression

But we would write:

- the age of reason, the nuclear age, the information age (lowercase).

Don't capitalize titles or other terms unless used in direct address:

Wrong:

- I saw the President of the United States.
- I have a Master's Degree in Philosophy.
- He is a Doctor in that hospital.

Correct:

- I saw President Obama but I never saw the secretary of state.
- I have a master's degree in philosophy.
- He is a doctor in that hospital.

A CAPITAL THOUGHT

A lot of authors are unclear regarding when to capitalize a title or profession. The rule is pretty simple. When you are using names of affection, like honey, sweetie, sis, etc., you keep them lowercase. When using titles in direct address, you capitalize them.

Example:

- I don't understand, Doctor.
- Will you tell me, Captain, when we will get there?
- Your tests are too hard, Professor.
- I talked to Mom today.
- You are great, King Richard.
- I know, Father. I should study harder.

And please note the comma before each term or title. The meaning of the sentence may be quite different without that comma (compare that last example to "I know Father").

Here's one tip to help you know when to capitalize: If you see the word *the* (or another article) before the term, you lowercase that term.

Example:

- The doctor told me I was overweight.
- I spoke to the captain, and he said we were almost there.
- My professor is really tough.
- I talked to my mom today.
  You are great, my dear king Richard. [By adding adjectives in front of the noun, you follow the same rule]

TIP FOR FICTION WRITERS: **Don't overplay dialect or accents in dialog. Using spelling to show dialect and accents has been out of favor for a long time because we learned other ways to convey differences in speech and pronunciation. You don't want readers struggling to understand what a character is saying because you've thrown odd spellings at them. Instead, you want to convey dialect and accents almost instantly so readers can get on with the story.**

CAPPING THE HOLIDAYS

Most writers don't have any trouble knowing when to capitalize the major holidays, such as Easter and Christmas. But it can get a little fuzzy with some of the other holidays. And for good reason. There is little consistency in the "rules" for "capping the holidays." Without a handy list like this, writers may have to head to the punch bowl for another cup of eggnog!

Here are some other holidays and relative expressions and the correct ways to write them:

- Christmas Eve
- Christmas Eve Day [no *Chicago* rule but seems the prevailing style]
- New Year's Day
- New Year's Eve
- New Year's
- Martin Luther King Jr. Day [no comma and no Dr.]
- Happy New Year [most sources say to use caps unless you are talking generically about a new year and not the celebration]
- Valentine's Day [but, "be my valentine"]
- Presidents' Day [although AP leaves out the apostrophe]
- Veterans Day [you'd think it would follow the same rule as above, but no]
- Columbus Day [so why isn't it Columbus's Day, in keeping with the prevailing style?]
- Mother's Day [why isn't this one plural possessive like Presidents' Day? Are we only celebrating one mother? If so, whose?]
- Father's Day [same here]

If you want to get a bit more confused, you can argue whether to write Secretary's Day or Secretaries' Day. Are you honoring just one secretary in your office or all of them? Same goes for Boss's Day or Bosses' Day. I don't know when that holiday came into being, but I imagine after the secretaries were getting goodies and being taken out to lunch, the bosses felt left out.

I wonder if anyone's come up with Bloggers' Day yet? I could use that box of chocolates right now!

NOTES

NOTES

NOTES

NUMBERS

NUMBERS AND NUMERALS COUNT

A few handy rules about numbers and numerals:

- Don't put the letter *A* in front of numeric values. Don't say, "A 127 people chose option b," or "the suit cost a $100." Just say, "There were 127 people who chose option b," or "the suit cost $100."

Be aware, too, that you can't begin a sentence with a numeral:

- Wrong: "127 people chose option B."
- Correct: "One hundred and twenty people chose option B" OR "A total of 127 people chose option B."

The second choice is really better because you really aren't supposed to spell out numbers over a hundred.

Some editors argue that numerals shouldn't be used in dialog because people don't "speak" in numerals, but there is nothing objectionable, according to *Chicago* style, that prevents a writer from using numerals in dialog. The main concern is you want to be clear and consistent.

No one wants to read a sentence like this:

- "Hey, I got seventeen thousand, eight hundred, and fifty-six downloads on Amazon."

This is so much easier on the eyes:

- "Hey, I saw you had 236 five-star reviews on Amazon—that's great," she said.

Chicago recommends using numerals for dates and in brand names like 7-Eleven.

- "I graduated class of '96." (Make sure your curly quote curves like a backward *c*.)
- "Let's ride down to 7-Eleven and get eight hot dogs."

Also be mindful when writing monetary values. Don't write "$100 dollars," just "$100." You have already implied *dollars* by using the $ sign.

The *CMOS* rule is to spell out numbers less than 101, as well as large round numbers, such as two hundred fifty and one thousand.

WHAT TIME IS IT?

I see a lot of confusion about when to spell out the time of day and when to show it as numerals. The rules are pretty simple. You want to spell out times of day if they are in even, half, or quarter hours:

- She left at seven o'clock and returned at seven fifteen.

If you want to stipulate a time of day that doesn't follow this rule, use the numerals:

- He looked at the clock and it read 6:18.

Now, if you really want to emphasize an *exact* time, you *can* use numerals even with times that normally would be spelled out:

- The store opens at exactly 8:30.

As far as dates go, just use the numeral and don't make it an ordinal:

- He's coming on December 5. (Not December 5th. Or you can spell out *fifth*.)

If you are not mentioning the month with the day, you spell out the day:

- She should be here on the sixteenth.

TIP FOR FICTION WRITERS: Most authorities will insist that every number should be spelled out when spoken in dialog, but some state it really doesn't matter. Amy Einsohn, in her excellent book *The Copy Editor's Handbook*, says, ". . . Some authors feel strongly about [always spelling out numbers in speech], arguing that speakers speak in words, not numerals. Although the logic of this argument is shaky—speakers speak sounds, which may be transcribed in various ways—copyeditors are usually expected to honor the author's preference in the matter."

TIME IS THE TOPIC OF THE DAY

Writers often refer to the time of day in a scene, so it's good to know when to spell out the time and when to use numerals. The rule is fairly simple. Times of day in even, half, and quarter hours are usually spelled out in text. With *o'clock*, the number is always spelled out.

- Her day begins at five o'clock in the morning.
- The meeting continued until half past three.
- He left the office at a quarter of four (or a quarter to four. The *a* before *quarter* is optional).
- We will resume at ten thirty.
- Cinderella almost forgot that she should leave the ball before midnight.

Numerals are used (with zeros for even hours) when exact times are emphasized. *Chicago* recommends lowercasing *a.m.* and *p.m.*, though these sometimes appear in small capitals, with or without periods.

- The first train leaves at 5:22 a.m. and the last at 11:00 p.m.
- She caught the 6:20 p.m. flight.
- Please attend a meeting in Grand Rapids, Michigan, on December 5 at 10:30 a.m.

> *TIP FOR FICTION WRITERS:* **Writers are sometimes guilty of using hedge words—*seemed, sort of, kind of, perhaps, a bit*—rather than simply making assertions. The impact is almost always stronger without the hedge. Rather than saying, "She noticed that he seemed to be angry," try "She startled at his harsh words."**

> *TIP FOR FICTION WRITERS:* **"If you have any young friends who aspire to become writers, the second greatest favor you can do them is to present them with copies of *The Elements of Style*. The first greatest, of course, is to shoot them now, while they're happy." ~ Dorothy Parker**

THE 100 PERCENT SOLUTION

If you are writing a technical or scientific paper, you would use the % sign. But in general or nonscientific writing, spell out the word *percent*. Except at the beginning of a sentence, percentages are usually expressed in numerals. You never want to begin a sentence with a numeral, so either rewrite so that doesn't occur or spell out the number. Here are some good examples of correct usage:

- Fewer than 5 percent of readers buy books at an actual bookstore.
- With 90–95 percent of the work complete, we can relax.
- A 75 percent likelihood of winning is worth the effort.
- Her five-year certificate of deposit carries an interest rate of 5.9 percent.
- Only 20% of the ants were observed to react to the stimulus.
- The treatment resulted in a 20%–25% increase in reports of blindness.
- A 10 percent solution (no hyphen).

Percent, used as an adverb, is not interchangeable with the noun *percentage*:

- I know that 1 percent is a very small percentage.

Note also that no space should be put between the numeral and the symbol %.

> *TIP FOR FICTION WRITERS:* You may have been told that writers should never start a sentence with *and, yet, but,* or *however* (or other conjunctions or adverbs.) This something that a lot of English teachers are sticklers about. They tell us that this is, in reality, creating a sentence fragment. That's just plain false. There's absolutely nothing wrong with starting a sentence with these words. Or any other word, for that matter. Which is my point.

NOTES

NOTES

NOTES

NOUNS AND PRONOUNS

MASS NOUNS AND COUNT NOUNS

Amount and *number* (the nouns, not the verbs) often get misused. Amount is a mass noun, and you use it when talking about things you can't count:

- "There is a large amount of smog."

Number is used, well, for things you can number, so that should help you remember the rule.

- "I filed a number of lawsuits."

I could say I see "a huge *number* of instances in which writers misuse the word *amount*, and a large *amount* of misunderstanding surrounding these two words."

This issue of mass nouns versus count nouns gets a bit muddled when deciding whether to use *fewer* or *less than*. The traditional rule holds that *fewer* is used with expressions denoting things that can be counted (*fewer than three people*), while *less* is used with mass terms denoting things of you can measure (*less paper; less than a gallon of paint*).

However, *less* can be used idiomatically. *Less than* is used before a plural noun that denotes a measure of time, amount, or distance:

- less than three weeks
- less than $400
- less than twenty miles

Less is sometimes used with plural nouns in the expressions no less than (as in no less than fifty people signed up for the conference) and or less (as in explain this in ten words or less).

Less than can be interpreted as a kind of "benchmark." That's why some feel the sign occasionally seen at markets—"Less than 10 items"—can be construed as correct. The idea being that "10 items" is a benchmark you are measuring against, and so eight items would be less than that benchmark (a mass noun instead of a count noun). But no one is going to be confused if you say "There are less than [instead of fewer than] five people in the room." However, try to use fewer than when appropriate.

And speaking of less than: don't use over when you mean more than:

- Wrong: There are over a hundred people in this waiting room.
- Correct: There are more than a hundred people in this waiting room.

That's a mistake I see all the time in manuscripts. But we are all less than [not fewer than] perfect!

ERADICATING ZOMBIE NOUNS

Zombies are big in movies and TV these days. But zombie nouns have been the bane of good writers for much longer. We know zombies as dead or inanimate objects come to life. Zombie nouns, also known as abstract nouns, suck the life out of good writing. It happens when parts of speech—most often verbs and adjectives—get turned into nouns. We call it *nominalization.*

It's an easy enough process. You simply add a suffix like *ion, ate,* or *ize* to an adjective or verb and it becomes a noun.

- The verb *complete* becomes the noun *completion.*
- The verb *study* becomes the noun (gerund) *studying.*
- The adjectives *happy* and *sad* become the nouns *happiness* and *sadness.*

Nominalizing a verb or adjective doesn't always change its form. Some verbs can function as nouns or verbs.

- Will you fix my computer? (verb)
- Yes, the fix is a simple reboot. (noun)

The verb form is the same, but how it's used changes. In the first sentence, *fix* is an action; in the second, it's a thing.

Turning a verb or adjective into a noun isn't always wrong, but as a practice it makes for wordy, passive writing, as these sentences illustrate:

- The detectives conducted an investigation of the murder.
- Change to: The detectives investigated the murder.

And:

- Holding our Christmas celebration on the Saturday before December 25 has been our practice for more than a decade.
- Change to: We have celebrated Christmas on the Saturday before December 25 for more than a decade.

To remedy nominalizations, look for nouns that can be turned into verbs. Nominalizations give more weight to the action than the person(s) responsible for them. A simple fix is locating the subject and verb and using that basic construction to breathe life back into your writing. Say no to zombie nouns!

TURNING VERBS INTO NOUNS MAY BE BAD FOR YOUR WRITING

Nominalization is a fancy word that means taking a part of speech such as a verb, adjective, or adverb and turning it into a noun—primarily at the head of a sentence. Doing this can lead to some weak sentence structure. So let's take a look at ways to identify and correct specific nominalizations, as well as point out some legitimate uses of nominalization.

Watch out for nominalizations that follow a verb:

- The auditors *conducted an investigation* into the embezzlement
- Better: The auditors *investigated* the embezzlement

Nominalization following *there is*:

- *There was an erosion* of customer confidence following the auditor's discovery.
- Better: The discovery *eroded* customers' confidence.

Nominalization as the subject of an empty verb:

- The partners' *discussion concerned* enhanced regulations.
- Better: The partners *discussed* enhanced regulations.

Consecutive nominalizations:

- *There was a* first *review* of the progression of the audit.
- Better: First, the partners *reviewed* the progression of the audit.
- Or: First, the partners *reviewed* how the audit progressed.
- Linked nominalizations:
- Their *insistence on* strict adherence to regulatory guidelines created the dilemma.
- Better: They *insisted* on adhering strictly to the regulatory guidelines, and it created the dilemma.

There are times when nominalization serves a legitimate purpose, such as to replace "the fact that":

- The fact that the auditors denied the claims of irresponsibility impressed the jurors.
- Better: The jurors were impressed that the auditors denied responsibility.

I hope this helps you spot those pesky nouns that work better if changed into verbs.

WHOM SHOULD YOU SAY?

No one, that's who! Maybe it sounds correct because you can picture someone prim and proper uttering these words, but to say "whom shall I say is calling" is grammatically incorrect. I struggle with this, and I'm sure others do too. I have to run through some mental gymnastics on occasion to remind myself when to use *who* and *whom*.

It's fairly straightforward. *Who* is for subjects and *whom* is for objects. You can replace *who* with a subject like *I, you,* or *he.* And you can replace *whom* with objective pronouns like *me* and *him.* Here are some correct examples for reference:

- Who made the birthday cake?
- Who is in the kitchen?
- Who is going to do the dishes?
- Whom are you going to invite?
- Whom did he blame for the accident?
- Whom did he hire to do the job?
- He doesn't know who the boss is
- She doesn't care whom you invite
- The man who called you is coming (simplify to "he is coming")
- I saw the woman whom you had spoken to (more succinct to leave out the whom)

More often than not, writers hypercorrect and use whom when they should just use *who*. Sometimes, though, it's just simpler and easier to rewrite.

TIP FOR FICTION WRITERS: **Don't overdo punctuation. Instead of using both an exclamation mark and a question mark to imply a character's intense emotion, let the words, context, and show of emotion bring the emphasis to the speech. A "rule" many editors and publishers have is "no more than three exclamation marks in a novel." Overdoing such marks is seen as a sign of weak or amateur writing.**

A HELPFUL WAY TO DETERMINE WHEN NOT TO USE "WHOM"

In another entry we looked at the phrase "Whom shall I say is calling?" and learned that such use of *whom* is incorrect. The trick to knowing whether to use *whom* or *who* in these instances is to remove the subject-verb combination that immediately follows the pronoun. Don't say "huh?" Let me show you.

With that famous phase, when you delete those words I mentioned, you would get this:

- "Whom is calling?"

You can always replace *whom* with *him* (object) or *who* with *he* (subject) to check if you are correct. Saying "him is calling" is not correct.

Watch what happens when I take out the subject-verb words in these sentences:

- The police have captured the man whom ~~they think~~ robbed the bank.
- The client hired the accountant whom ~~she remembered~~ was helpful.
- He didn't want to invite the woman, whom ~~his friend had said~~ was a bore.

Clearly, whom is wrong in these instances. That's because the pronoun (whom) connects to the action of that person (robbed, not think, in the first example), not the action of the subject of the sentence. (I tried to explain this in as simple a way as I can here, without getting too grammar techy. Stay with me . . .)

What helps me in these cases is to group those words together in my head:

- The man who robbed the bank.
- The accountant who was helpful.
- The woman who was a bore.

I hope this helps you understand *whom* better. I've been studying the advice of the grammar instructors *who* I feel know what they are talking about!

ARE YOU A WHO OR A THAT?

I sometimes get asked when to use *who* vs. *that* in a sentence. These two words are relative pronouns that need to correspond to the noun they're referring to.

Let's take this sentence: "The candidate who spends the most money usually wins the election."

Who connects the subject, *candidate*, to the verb *wins*.

Many people will say "The candidate that spends the most money usually wins the election."

Here's the thing: "who" (and its forms) refers to people. "That" usually refers to things, but it can refer to people in a general sense (like a class or type of person). Purdue Online Writing Lab says, "When referring to people, both *that* and *who* can be used in informal language. 'That' may be used to refer to the characteristics or abilities of an individual or a group of people. . . .

However, when speaking about a particular person in formal language, *who* is preferred."

That said, many people and some respected references prefer "people that," and it's not wrong. I often have animals that are main characters in my fantasy books, and they speak (proper English, most of the time). So, I choose to use *who* instead of *that*. But some stickler will insist animals aren't "whos." You decide.

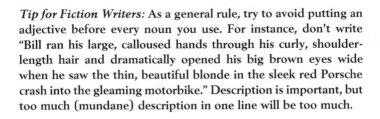

> *Tip for Fiction Writers:* As a general rule, try to avoid putting an adjective before every noun you use. For instance, don't write "Bill ran his large, calloused hands through his curly, shoulder-length hair and dramatically opened his big brown eyes wide when he saw the thin, beautiful blonde in the sleek red Porsche crash into the gleaming motorbike." Description is important, but too much (mundane) description in one line will be too much.

WHICH TO USE—WHICH OR THAT?

These two words are often used incorrectly, and it's not too hard to understand when you want *that* instead of *which*. *The* word *that* is used with what's called a restrictive clause—meaning the phrase that's following this word is necessary to the meaning of the sentence. For example:

- All the books that are about dogs are on that shelf. [This means every book about dogs is on the shelf.]
- I went to see the movie that had a lot of singing. [This means you specifically chose a movie with singing as opposed to another movie without singing.]
- He liked my novel that reminded him of home. [This means this novel reminded him of home as opposed to others, which didn't.]

Now, look at the difference in meaning by using *which* instead (and notice the offsetting commas). *Which* is used with a nonrestrictive clause, which means the phrase it's a part of isn't essential to the meaning but just adds something already known to the first phrase (I just gave you an example in this sentence).

- All the books, which are about dogs, are on that shelf. [This means all the books are on the shelf, and they just happen to be about dogs. The emphasis here is on the fact that the books are on the shelf. It doesn't really matter what they're about. The fact that they're about dogs is an additional bit of information that doesn't change the essential meaning of the sentence.]
- I went to see the movie, which had a lot of singing. [This means the singing isn't singling out which movie you saw. The movie you saw just happened to have singing, but it doesn't change the essential fact of the sentence—that you went to the movies.]
- He liked my novel, which reminded him of home. [This means he liked my novel not because it reminded him of home—he just liked it. And it also reminded him of home.]

In most instances, you are going to have a comma before *which*. That's because you are introducing a nonrestrictive bit of info. Some grammar gurus feel it's fine to interchange *which* and *that* in many circumstances, but if you follow this generally accepted, rule, you should do fine for the most part, which is a good goal to have (the *which* put here to emphasize my point!).

SUCH IS THE WAY OF PRONOUNS

We tend to default to "their" when following singular pronouns, which is bad, bad, bad. Or so many say. Some pronouns are singular, and so the verbs following them must be singular, as in "Nobody knows what trouble I've seen." Seems intuitive—until you get to those sentences like "Everybody grabbed their backpacks [did they each grab one or more than one?] and headed for the door."

Be aware that there are some pronouns that can be either singular or plural depending on the intent. Here are some examples:

- Such is the way of the fool.
- Such are the ways of the world.
- None is as stupid as I am.
- None are expected to make it down that mountain alive.
- Any is fine with me.
- Any of these foods are healthy.
- Some of that pudding has turned green; don't eat it.
- Some are really dumb to eat green pudding.
- All of that pie looks good to me.
- All are waiting eagerly for you to cut the cake.

Hmm, maybe you can tell I'm writing this around dinnertime; I'm thinking of food examples. But I hope you get the point. Just use your pronouns carefully! (And really—avoid that green pudding!)

TIP FOR FICTION WRITERS: Be sure to use your character's name right away in a scene. Don't use a pronoun and keep the reader guessing whom you are talking about (unless you are being very deliberate about creating a mystery). But once you do name your POV character, don't keep using the name over and over. Just say "he" or "she" unless you need to be clear whom you are referring to (in scenes with other characters).

SOMEONE HAS THEIR PRONOUNS GOOFY

It's sometimes hard to make sense of whether certain pronouns are singular or plural, so here are some helpful explanations. The indefinite pronouns *anyone, anybody, everyone, everybody, someone, somebody, no one,* and *nobody* are always singular. This is sometimes confusing to writers who feel that *everyone* and *everybody* (especially) are referring to more than one person. The same is true of *either* and *neither*, which are always singular even though they seem to be referring to two things.

The need for pronoun-antecedent agreement can create gender problems. If you were to write, for instance, "A student must see his counselor before the end of the semester" when there are female students involved, nothing but grief will follow. You can pluralize, in this situation, to avoid the problem:

- Students must see their counselor before the end of the semester.
- Or, you could say:
- A student must see his or her counselor . . . [which to me is a bit unattractive]

Using *his* and *hers* repeatedly eventually becomes annoying, however, and the reader becomes more aware of the writer trying to be conscious of good form than he or she is of the matter at hand (see how clunky that sounds?).

Trying to conform to the above rule can lead to a great deal of nonsense. It's widely regarded as being correct (or correct enough) to say, "Somebody has put their notebook on the table." But many people would object its being written that way because *somebody* is singular and *their* is plural. There's a great deal to be said, however, for using the word *their* as the gender-nonspecific, singular pronoun.

Remember that when we compound a pronoun with something else, we don't want to change its form. Following this rule carefully often creates something that "doesn't sound good." You would write, "This food is for me," so when a person (or object) is added into the mix, don't write, "This food is for Fred and I."

Try these:

- This money is for him and me.
- This arrangement is between Fred and him.

The best way to figure out if you've written it correctly is to take one of the people out and just say, "This money is for me." If it's sounds right, it's right.

CLEAR AND PRESENT ANTECEDENTS

Pronouns take the place of nouns. When you use a pronoun, you must be sure that its antecedent (what it refers to) is clear. For instance, who does *her* refer to in this sentence?

- Both Heidi and Mary loved her children.

Her is an unclear antecedent because we don't know if it refers to Heidi's children or Mary's children.

So let's look at one word that can be a little tricky: *other*. It's one of those words that serves multiple roles in our language—noun, pronoun, adjective, or adverb. But for our purposes right now, let's look at its role as a pronoun.

You've probably read a sentence like this a hundred times and never given it much thought:

- Jesse's artwork has been displayed in the Omaha Public Library, Creighton University, and the governor's mansion, among others.

Then again, you may have wondered, "among other whats?" Here *others* does not have a clear antecedent. It's a pronoun without a noun. What do the proper nouns in this sentence have in common? They are venues, but that hasn't been defined in this sentence. So to be clear, the sentence could be recrafted in one of these ways:

- Jesse's artwork has been displayed in the Omaha Public Library, Creighton University, and the governor's mansion, among other venues.

In this variation, *other* is an adjective describing venues. Another option is to insert the noun *venues* earlier in the sentence:

- Jesse's artwork has been displayed in venues like the Omaha Public Library, Creighton University, and the governor's mansion, among others.

Now it is clear that *among others* refers to venues. A similar construction avoids the problem completely:

- He has created artwork for doctors, lawyers, politicians, and others.

Here there is no ambiguity because *others* is a noun like its antecedents "doctors, lawyers, and politicians." I trust we can all agree on that.

So take a moment to look through your manuscript and check those pronouns. Make sure you have a clear antecedent.

DO YOU SPEAK TO EACH OTHER OR ONE ANOTHER?

Sometimes people are confused about when to use *each other* and *one another.* Well, there's a good reason for the confusion. Even the people who make up the rules—the grammarians—don't agree on this one.

So let's start with the things they do agree on:

Each other and *one another* are pronouns (used in place of nouns). They are reciprocal pronouns. That means that both individuals experience the same thing; it's a mutual relationship.

- Bill and Sue love each other.
- Unfortunately, their parents couldn't stand each other.

Both the affection and the dislike go both ways. Use *each other* when talking about two people.

Be sure to note the context and what you intend. For instance, when you're speaking or writing about an event that has a clear order or stages, *one another* is the preferred usage.

- One after another the contestants filed past the judges.
- The children followed one another to the playground.

While it would not be wrong to say "The children followed each other to the playground," *one another* is preferred.

One grammarian suggests that this is a style preference rather than a matter of correctness. The wise approach is to follow the rule, even though there really is little rationale for it.

When used as possessive pronouns, the noun that follows is almost always plural.

- The parents really got on each other's nerves.

Here's an exception:

- They couldn't even stand the sound of one another's voice. [Because each parent has only one voice, obviously, the noun following the possessive pronoun is singular.]

Each other and *one another* should never be used as the subjects of a clause.

Let's say Bill thinks Sue is the perfect mate, and Sue thinks the same of Bill. Saying or writing "Bill and Sue think each other are the perfect mate" is awkward, if not incorrect. Bill and Sue each think the other is the perfect mate. Separating the pronoun actually puts each in its proper place. This is one time when separating a pair is a good thing.

MORE LIKE ME OR I

Do you look more like me . . . or do you look more like I? The case of a pronoun following this kind of comparative structure, typically at the end of a sentence, depends on who or what is being compared.

If you write "My sister looks more like our father than I," for example, one would assume that the "I" implies "I do." But you wouldn't fault someone for thinking you mean your sister looks more like your father than like you. This is often a source of confusion, so it's best to reword for clarity. If the point is whether the sister looks more like the father, the pronoun should be in the objective case (*me*, not *I*): my sister looks more like our father than she looks like me.

Instead of writing "My sister looks more like our father than me," I might rewrite "My sister looks more like our father than like me." That pretty much eliminates the problem. And if you add the word *do* to that first example, you won't have any confusion either: ""My sister looks more like our father than I do."

Tip for Fiction Writers: Writers should avoid clichés in their writing, but that doesn't mean certain characters shouldn't think and/or speak using clichés. Give colorful characters "pet" phrases or clichés that make them memorable. I recall one character from the TV series *LA Law* that continually said, "Correct me if I'm wrong." That character and phrase have stuck with me for years!

Tip for Fiction Writers: Rules in grammar, especially in fiction, can't always be hard and fast, as much as we'd like them to be. Carol Fisher Saller, editor of the *CMOS* Q &A section, says, "A need to always cleave to the rules can be counterproductive. . . . [sometimes] it's not a matter of being correct or incorrect. It's only a style." Try to learn, though, which are styles and which are rules that should be adhered to.

NOTES

NOTES

NOTES

VERBS AND ADVERBS

TO LAY OR TO LIE—THAT IS THE QUESTION

If I were asked to vote on the verb that causes the most confusion and is invariably conjugated incorrectly more often than correctly, *lie* would win hands down. If you Google "to lie" or "lay/lie" you can find enough websites discussing these seemingly unobtrusive, simple words to fill volumes.

How can a three-letter word cause so much grief? I think there are two reasons. 1) the word *lay* has two completely different uses and 2) we use these verbs incorrectly in speech as well. I am guilty of often saying something like, "The dog's laying on the couch." I often hear people using *lay* instead of *lie*. But what's even more "off" to me are the "creative" conjugations some people come up with like:

(And please note: these are wrong!)

- I lied on the couch for six hours (wow, your voice must have gone hoarse talking for so long!).
- I layed down when I got tired.
- The chicken layed an egg.

Really, there are only six words you need to remember. If you recite them a bunch of times, you might just be able to recall them when you need them. And two of them repeat, so you really only need to know four words. How hard is that? Here they are:

- Lie, lay, lain
- Lay, laid, laid

If you're not sure when to use *lie*, think of *recline* (Hear the long *i* sound in both words). *Lie* (not the verb discussing whether you are telling the truth or not) is something you do to yourself—you lie down. I lie down today. I lay down yesterday. I had lain down every day for a week.

Lay is something you do to something else (in grammar-talk this verb takes a direct object. *Lie* never does). When you think of *lay*, think of *place* (Hear the long *a* sound in both words). I lay the book on the table. I laid the book on the table. I had laid the book on the table every day this week.

So just repeat after me: "Lie, lay, lain. Lay, laid, laid . . ."

I think I need to go lie down now.

TENSES DON'T HAVE TO BE INTENSE

You took those English grammar classes in school, and you really don't want to suffer through them again, do you? To be a great fiction writer, you don't have to memorize all the parts of speech and be able to spout off all the various tenses. So take a deep breath and calm down. But know this—it does help to understand how words function in a sentence, and yes, it's good to know a little about tenses.

But learning about tenses doesn't have to be intense. When you study a foreign language, you often learn a lot about your own because you're called upon to learn the various tenses and know how to conjugate verbs. And it's good to understand tenses when you're a fiction writer because you won't always be writing in present tense.

I see a lot of problems with tenses in the manuscripts I critique and edit. Often writers mix their tenses up or don't use the proper one for the passage they are writing. I often query writers with comments like: "Do you mean this is happening now? Or did you mean for this to be in the past?" This can cause huge problems in your story, so it would be wise to make sense of tenses.

Here's a simple breakdown of the most common tenses:

- Present tense, happening now: I walk down the street. [That was easy, right?]
- Past tense, over and done with: I walked down the street. [Still easy, right?]

Now here's a group of tenses that are called "perfect." Why are they perfect—are they better than all the rest? No, silly. They are perfect because they are complete, done, finished.

- Present Perfect: I have walked down the street. [Done, over]
- Past Perfect: I had walked down the street. [Before something else happened]

If you want to go for the big one, here it is:

- Future Perfect: I will have walked down the street. [an action that will be complete in the future]

Is that all the tenses? Oh heavens, no. But I hope you now understand perfectly the perfect tenses. I have finished (present perfect) giving you my lesson.

ARE YOU PROGRESSIVELY TENSE?

It's important for fiction writers to understand what progressive tense is. Why? Because it's used too often and can weaken your writing. So if you know what it is, you can look out for it (kind of like digging out the bits of onion in your salad you don't like). We tend to use this tense casually in speech in writing, and it certainly has its place. But if it's not needed or just the right tense required for what you mean to say, then replace it with a better tense.

Certain tenses are progressive because they indicate things that are in the middle of happening. They are not completed (perfect, as in perfect tenses) yet. Here are some examples:

- Present Progressive: I am walking down the street. [This tense is formed with the verb "to be."]
- Past Progressive: I was walking down the street. [Notice the *ing* at the end of these verbs. That's a signal you're dealing with a progressive tense.]
- Future Progressive: I will be walking down the street.

So why is the progressive (sometimes called "passive") tense a bad thing *sometimes*? Because you want to try to have your characters be more active and not so passive.

Want to challenge yourself? See if you can now figure out what Present *Perfect* Progressive would look like (no peeking below).

Okay, here it is:

- I have been walking down the street all day.

And here are the other Perfect versions of the Progressive tense:

- Past Perfect Progressive: I had been walking down the street. [Note the shift from *have* to *had* when talking about the past.]
- Future Perfect Progressive: I will have been walking down the street. [Starts sounding a bit clunky . . .]

So you can see how this tense can get not only passive but cluttered, which could make you progressively tense. Makes sense these are called progressive tenses. If you can find these in your writing and change them to the simple present or past tense, your writing may come across more concise and clear, which is a good thing.

For example: Instead of writing "Bill was walking down the street," say "Bill walked down the street." Unless you need to explain that Bill was walking down the street when something happened.

MORE VERBS TO DRUG YOU THROUGH

Here are some lines that are similar to many I see in manuscripts I edit:

- "After George drug Ralph through the mud, he sunk into his easy chair and watched TV."
- "The sun shined on the water after the sun had rose."
- "I sung a song after I swum across the lake, then I drunk a bottle of beer."

Okay, I hope you saw some problems in these sentences. If you didn't, that's okay. That's why you're reading this book—to improve your grammar, right? So, don't feel bad—you're not alone.

If you want to get technical, what is happening is writers are using the past participle form (usually with had, as in "I had swum") with the past indicative (the "regular old" past tense, as in "I swam.") So here are the three correct forms of some verbs you may sometimes get confused (present, past, and past participle forms):

- Swim, swam, swum
- Shine, shined, shined (if you are shining shoes or some object)
- Shine, shone, shone (if an object is shining on its own, such as the sun)
- Rise, rose, risen (the sun had risen at six a.m.)
- Raise, raised, raised (as in lifting your arm)
- forbid, forbade, forbidden
- Get, got, gotten
- Bear, bore, borne (carry)
- Bare, bared, bared (reveal)
- Drink, drank, drunk
- Hang, hanged, hanged (as in swinging from the gallows)
- Hang, hung, hung (to suspend)
- Shake, shook, shaken

And it's drag, dragged, dragged—no, not drugged. That involves chemicals. Which makes me think of another entry in this book that deals with the misuse of lie and *lay*. "I lied on the bed after they drugged me there." Some writers intend for this to mean they were reclining on the bed after someone pulled them along the floor. But I'm sure you see how this really means something entirely different (more like an abduction scene from a spy thriller, right?).

YOU WOKE ME . . . OR DID YOU WAKE ME?

These verbs often mess me up, so I thought I'd share them with you.

This is how to conjugate the verb *to sink*: sink, sank, sunk (I too often see writers using *sunk* instead of *sank*):

- I sink
- I sank
- I had sunk into the water

(*To drink* follows the same pattern.)

This is how you conjugate *to wake*: wake, woke, waken (or woken):

- I wake
- I woke up
- I had waken (woken)

Or you may choose this route . . . awaken, awoke, awaked (or awakened):

- I awaken [wake up]
- I awoke [woke up]
- I had awaked (awakened) [waked up]

Is this starting to get as muddled to you as it is to me?

I think I've awakened to a sunk feeling . . . I mean, a sinking feeling . . .

TIP FOR FICTION WRITERS: One paragraph, one idea. Many people write inordinately long paragraphs that contain multiple ideas or assertions, and stretch across multiple pages. A paragraph should contain one idea. When writing narrative, you should usually lead with a topic sentence, and the rest of the paragraph should be an elaboration on that sentence. If you find yourself moving to a new topic, start a new paragraph.

HOW MUCH FURTHER?

The adverbs *farther* and *further* are often a problem for many writers. It helps me to think of *farther* as only applying to actual distance, but you would say, "We cannot travel any *further* tonight" if you are talking about physical distance. *Farther* is used to note the progression of physical distance. "I ran *farther* than I ever had before."

Further seems to cover everything else:

- Thoughts of leaving are furthest from my mind.
- Let's discuss this further.
- The farther we go into the desert, the hotter it gets.
- I am farther away from the store than you are.
- I am further from realizing my goals than I was last year.
- Stop before you go any further on that topic.

If you're dealing with a sentence that seems a bit ambiguous, you really can use either word. People regularly use either word for physical distance, and it's become acceptable. But to be safe, default to *further* and you'll probably be fine. No need to fret further on the subject.

TIP FOR FICTION WRITERS: Author Stephen King states: "The adverb is not your friend. Consider the sentence 'He closed the door firmly.' It's by no means a terrible sentence, but ask yourself if *firmly* really has to be there. What about context? What about all the enlightening (not to say emotionally moving) prose which came *before* 'He closed the door firmly'? Shouldn't this tell us how he closed the door? And if the foregoing prose *does* tell us, then isn't *firmly* an extra word? Isn't it redundant?"

ARE YOU SINGULAR?

Sometimes using singular verbs sounds wrong, but we're back to the rules again. When you use a singular noun, your verb needs to be singular. Take a look at the *correct* sentences and see whether you would have written them correctly.

- "My favorite type of movie is thrillers," but "Thrillers are my favorite type of movie."
- "Neither is correct." (And, just as in the above example, the presence of a modifier is irrelevant. You would write: "Neither of them is correct.")
- "The pot of eggs is boiling on the stove."
- "Either the dog or the cats are responsible for the mess." ("Either the cats or the dog is responsible for the mess" is also technically correct but is awkward.)
- "His staff is assembled," but "Staff are asked to go to the conference room immediately." (In the first sentence, the emphasis is on the body of employees; in the second sentence, the focus is on compliance by each individual in the body of employees.)
- "The United Nations is headquartered in New York."
- "The economics of the situation are complicated," but "Economics is a complicated topic."
- "I am one of those eccentrics who do not tweet." (The verb goes with the noun: eccentrics. Think "those who do not tweet")
- "I am the only one of my friends who does not tweet." (think "one who does not tweet")
- "The number of people here boggles the mind." (number is singular)

Clearly, there is no singular rule about singularity. Alas.

TIP FOR FICTION WRITERS: **To keep your scenes from being tedious to read, break up long paragraphs. Every time there is a shift in focus, such as the character's attention moving from one person or thing to another, use a paragraph break. A variety of paragraph lengths will help with pacing.**

DO YOU SMELL BAD OR BADLY?

Here's something that writers often mix up. When you use verbs that express a state of being rather than an action, like become, feel, seem, smell, sound, taste, you follow them with an adjective, so they are not treated like adverbs. Do you remember the rule about adverbs—they usually have ly at the end? Here's how you use these types of verbs:

- I am fine, he became sad, she feels bad [not badly], they felt ill, you seem happy.

If you say "the fish smells bad," you mean it stinks. If you say "the fish smells badly," it means the fish has a poor sense of smell.

If you say "I feel bad," it means you are sad or sorry. If you say "I feel badly," it means your fingers are not very sensitive, and you can't tell what you are touching.

If you say "I look different than you," it means we don't look alike. But if I say "I look differently than you," it means my way of looking is not the same as your way.

I hope you are thinking differently now about all these touchy-feely things!

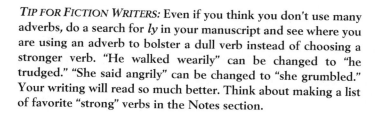

TIP FOR FICTION WRITERS: Even if you think you don't use many adverbs, do a search for *ly* in your manuscript and see where you are using an adverb to bolster a dull verb instead of choosing a stronger verb. "He walked wearily" can be changed to "he trudged." "She said angrily" can be changed to "she grumbled." Your writing will read so much better. Think about making a list of favorite "strong" verbs in the Notes section.

NOTES

NOTES

NOTES

ADJECTIVES

ARE YOU COORDINATING?

I think one of the more subtle problems in punctuation is in understanding a coordinate adjective and when to use a comma. It's up to you to determine if the adjectives describing a noun are coordinate or "equal" in their description. If so, you need a comma. A trick to figuring out if you need a comma is to say the sentence a different way. Here's what I do:

First, the sentence: I have a thick wide green book.

I then say, "I have a book that is green, wide, and thick." Wide and thick are similar adjectives, but green describes the book in a different manner. In fact, I have a green book that is thick and wide. That means I would punctuate the sentence like this:

"I have a thick, wide green book." You don't want to separate the noun from the immediate adjective with a comma.

Wrong:

- A big, house
- An angry, African lion
- A tall wide building [tall and wide are similar types of adjectives so you need the comma]

There are two "tests" to see if a pair of adjectives is coordinate: Use a comma if you can place *and* between them, and if you can reverse the order.

- I have a horrible, pounding headache.
- I have a horrible and pounding headache.
- I have a pounding and horrible headache.

To me, this sounds funny, so I would not use a comma:

- I have a horrible pounding headache.

But this sounds right:

- He raced a sleek, shiny boat.
- He raced a sleek and shiny boat.
- He raced a shiny and sleek boat.

Sometimes it's not quite clear if adjectives are coordinate, but if you restructure the sentence a few different ways, you should be able to tell. I like the example discussed in *The Copy Editor's Handbook* (Amy Einsohn): A battered old canvas fishing hat. Because none of the adjectives is coordinate, you don't need a comma anywhere. Can you tell?

THE MARCH OF THE ADJECTIVES

Adjectives add color to writing. In case you forgot what an adjective is, they are those words that modify or describe a noun (thing). Because they describe nouns, it's not unusual to use more than one before a noun. But I bet you didn't you know there is an "acceptable" way to order these adjectives.

Oftentimes a certain order sounds better, but we're hard-pressed to explain why. I sometimes stop editing when I come across a line like "he wore a black long coat." It just feels wrong to put *black* before *long*. Our language has developed such that certain adjectives just sound better in a certain order. It has nothing to do with a hierarchy of importance, and no, you don't organize alphabetically. It's likely that these general rules are somewhat ingrained in us, and that's why our ear is accustomed to putting adjectives in a certain order without knowing the reason.

The general rule is that *opinion* adjectives precede *fact* adjectives.

- The quick [opinion] brown [fact] fox jumps over the lazy dog.

Interesting. I wonder why that's so.

Within the category of fact adjectives, grammarians have established a preferred order:

- Size, shape, age, color
- Origin
- Material
- Purpose

That explains "the old gray [material?] mare."

Consider this: The tall [size] Russian [origin] woman set her dish on the wide [size] oblong [shape] old [age] blue [color] plastic [material] party [purpose] tablecloth.

Extra credit (if you've read the entry on coordinate adjectives): Where would you put commas, if any, in the above sentence? Answer: Probably only between *wide* and *oblong,* since size and shape are similar types (coordinate) adjectives. Really. Here's how you'd write it:

- The tall Russian woman set her dish on the wide, oblong old blue plastic party tablecloth.

It's important to note that not all grammarians agree on this order, and the rules are not rigid. Sometimes the order may be rearranged for emphasis.

- I'd like to buy a silk square scarf. (My first preference is that it be silk; shape is secondary.)

WATCH OUT FOR SUPERFLUOUS ADJECTIVES

A little goes a long way when it comes to adjectives. And you *can* have too much of a good thing sometimes.

While adjectives help your readers get a clearer picture of the person or thing you want them to see, not every adjective is essential. Eliminating one may improve a sentence.

Here's an example:

- The expedition climbed the high mountain.

No need for that adjective in front of mountain; we know mountains are high.

- Three-year-old Davis cheered for the brave superhero.

Bravery is one of the characteristics that makes a superhero a superhero. Strong nouns don't need the assistance of an adjective.

How about this:

- The furry cat chased the small mouse into a dark hole in the ground.

Do those superfluous adjectives make for interesting writing? I think not.

Be on the lookout for redundant adjectives, especially when you have a strong, descriptive noun. Marketers use this ploy to make their product seem more enticing—"more organic, tasty, beautiful, more [fill in the blank]." Beyond the "new and improved" line, see if you can spot empty adjectives that really don't add anything to what you need to know about a product. Like "garden vegetable" or "natural minerals."

As I often tell my editing clients: less is more. Taking the time to choose just the right adjective will often preclude the need for a second (or third). Stuffing a lot of words into a manuscript to give it life and make it exciting often gives the opposite effect. So don't be superfluous. That word comes from Latin, meaning to overflow. We don't want to flood our readers with adjectives. Just sprinkle them into your writing instead, and your sentences won't drown from weightiness.

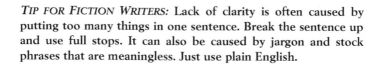

> *TIP FOR FICTION WRITERS:* Lack of clarity is often caused by putting too many things in one sentence. Break the sentence up and use full stops. It can also be caused by jargon and stock phrases that are meaningless. Just use plain English.

EACH AND EVERY WAY TO GET CONFUSED

Let's talk about *each* and *every*.

Grammarians call them quantifiers, which is just a highfalutin word that means number or quantity. *Each* and *every* are used to indicate quantity. But neither indicates a specific number. So, while their meanings are similar, the words are not always interchangeable.

Use *each* when you're referring to the persons or items in a group individually; use *every* when you consider the group as a unit.

- Each member of the team received a ribbon for participating.
- Every ribbon was green.

Use each when there are two persons or items; use every for groups of three or more.

- Two members of the team were named as scholar-athletes. Each rejoiced at the honor.
- Every team member congratulated them.

It is never correct to use *every* when there are only two items.

- The honorees carried an award in each [not every] hand. (You could say "in both hands.")

When there are more than two objects, either *each* or *every* is acceptable.

- The coach congratulated each/every parent. (Parent is the object, and there are multiple sets of parents. The coach congratulated all of them.)

Use every to indicate how often something happens. In the following examples, there are more than two options for when something occurs, so the correct adjective is *every*—never *each*.

- Soccer is played every fall.
- The games are played every weekend.

A SIMPLE, FUN LESSON ABOUT PARTICIPIAL PHRASES

Now, don't get all hot and bothered by the expression "participial phrase." Something that is *participial* has to do with the part of speech that is a participle. What's a participle? Well, it's complicated. Let's just say it reminds me of a photon—which can be both a particle and a wave.

In similar fashion, a participle can be a kind of verb and an adjective. How? By forming a phrase with a verb, you create a kind of adjective that modifies (affects, alters, describes) a noun.

One telltale sign of an inexperienced writer is the overuse of participial phrases to begin a sentence. Participial phrases are easily identified because they almost always begin with a verb that ends in *ing* or *ed.* If the participle is in present tense, it will dependably end in *ing.* Likewise, a regular past participle will end in a consistent *ed.* Irregular past participles, unfortunately, conclude in all kinds of ways.

Ask yourself how much of the information delivered through the participial phrases is necessary to the narrative.

- Seething with anger, Jennifer stormed into the kitchen. Slamming the door, she shouted for her mother. Finding her in the living room, she demanded, "How could you? Telling Mrs. Olson about my crush on Jimmy."

See which you think is more concise and less clunky:

- *Eaten by mosquitoes*, we wished that we had made hotel, not campsite, reservations.
- We wished we had stayed in a hotel instead of a campsite. The mosquitoes ate us alive.

Or this:

- The water drained slowly in the pipe *clogged with dog hair.*
- The pipe was so clogged with dog hair, the water barely drained.

You can see how awkward using these participial phrases are. I sometimes see manuscripts that are chock-full of them (Interesting aside: *chock-full* comes from the Middle English word that means "to choke." So don't let these phrases choke your writing).

It's a good practice to review your writing for any unnecessary participles and remove them, or find another way to convey that important piece of the narrative. If you're a photon, you can decide if you want to be a particle or a wave. If you're a writer, you can decide if you want to turn verbs into adjectives. Sometimes it's not a good idea.

MORE WAYS TO GET EACH AND EVERY CONFUSED

Here's the tricky thing. Each and every go with singular nouns. And because of this, they take a singular verb, with one exception.

- Each member of the team is responsible for keeping up morale. (Each=singular subject; is=singular verb.)
- Every boy is doing his best to comply. (boy=singular subject; every=adjective describing boy; is=singular verb.)

Here's the exception: when *each* serves as an appositive to a plural subject, the verb becomes plural. What is an appositive? Something that relates to the subject being discussed.

- The coaches each have written a letter of congratulations to the boys' parents. (Coaches=plural, each amplifies coaches; have=plural verb).

Here's an alternative way of writing this:

- Each of the coaches has written a letter of congratulations to the boys' parents.

Here *each* becomes the singular subject, requiring the singular verb *has written*.

And here's something else to keep in mind: *Each* can be used as a pronoun (replacing a noun), but *every* cannot:

- The soccer players waited eagerly for the awards to be announced; each was on edge.
- The soccer players waited eagerly for the awards to be announced; every one of them was on edge.

Each replaces players, but *every* does not. *Every* must be followed by a noun, or in this case, the noun phrase—*one of them.*

I've covered quite a few instances of when and how to use *each* and *every* correctly, although likely not each and every one.

TIP FOR FICTION WRITERS: "Increase your word power. Words are the raw material of our craft. The greater your vocabulary the more effective your writing. We who write in English are fortunate to have the richest and most versatile language in the world. Respect it." ~ P. D. James

LEARNING ABOUT PROPER ADJECTIVES IN A NEW YORK MINUTE

A "proper adjective" does not refer to a correct adjective in a sentence (because there often isn't just one correct adjective). It is one that, being or deriving from a proper name, always begins with a capital letter. Here are some examples of a proper adjective:

- a New York minute
- a Cuban cigar
- a Canadian dollar

The proper name used attributively (meaning the adjective is describing the noun, essentially) is still capitalized, but it does not cause the noun it modifies to be capitalized.

A place-name containing a comma—such as Toronto, Ontario, or New Delhi, India—should generally not be used as an adjective because a second comma may be deemed obligatory.

For example if you say, "We ate dinner in a Chicago, Illinois, restaurant," the comma after *Illinois* is somewhat awkward. Better to reword to something like "We ate dinner in a restaurant in Chicago, Illinois." Or "We ate dinner in a Chicago restaurant."

TIP FOR FICTION WRITERS: **Make sure your characters keep all body parts attached. A gaze can follow a person and so can a stare, but if someone's eyes follow? Can you have a character throw her eyes across the room (ugh)? Watch out for lines like: "Her eyes flew to the other end of the kitchen," and "His head followed her across the room."**

TIP FOR FICTION WRITERS: **"Every writer knows fear and discouragement. Just write. The world is crying for new writing. It is crying for fresh and original voices and new characters and new stories. If you won't write the classics of tomorrow, well, we will not have any." ~ Anne Rice**

NOTES

NOTES

OTHER PARTS OF SPEECH

NOT ALWAYS "AS" YOU "LIKE" IT

Do you recall the 1950s' cigarette commercial jingle that went like this: "Winston tastes good, like a cigarette should"? I know this dates me, but I do. I also recall being told in school that this sentence is grammatically incorrect.

If you're like me, you struggle a bit with *like* and *as*. Why? Because in modern usage, using *like* instead of *as* has become almost accepted and integrated into modern language. On Garner's scale of 1-5 (*Garner's Modern American Usage*), with 5 indicating a word or phrase has become "universally accepted," he rates this usage as a 4.

Grammatical purists insist that using *like* as a conjunction rather than a preposition breaks the rule. The rule they are referring to states that *like* is a preposition that functions as an adjective, not an adverb, and must be followed by a noun or pronoun. *As* or *as if* is a conjunction. Conjunctions connect clauses. Hence, grammarians cringed at the ad, claiming that in the offending line, *like* functions as a conjunction joining an independent clause—"Winston tastes good"—with a subordinate clause—"a cigarette should taste."

When *like* is used as a preposition it means "similar to" or "typical of." Notice how you could replace *like* with *similar to* in the following examples:

- Alice looks like her mother.
- Her dress looked like an original Donna Karan.

A common mistake is using *like* when *as if* is what's called for:

- It looks ~~like~~ as if the government shutdown is about to come to an end.
- Joan looks ~~like~~ as if she has lost her best friend.

In both examples, as if functions as a conjunction connecting two independent clauses. However—and do keep this in mind—when writing fiction, there are occasions (sometimes a lot of them!) when a character is going to think and speak inaccurately, based on who he is, his background, or his education. In many manuscripts I critique and edit, I allow the writer to break this rule because I can tell the characters would break certain grammatical rules. And you must always keep characters in character!

BETWEEN I OR ME?

I see this a lot, and from what I've researched, objective case confuses some people. It does me too. A quickie grammar lesson: When you have a subject of a sentence, you'll often find an object somewhere near or at the end.

For instance, the sentence "He passed the food to me" has *he* as the subject and *me* as the object. In this sentence: "He passed the food between us," the word *us* is in the objective (think *object*) case. We don't say, "He passed the food between we." *We* is in the subjective (subject) case. So if you put on your thinking cap, which is the correct sentence below?

- Just between you and I, I think the guy's nuts.
- Just between you and me, I think the guy's nuts.

If you said the second one is correct, you're right. Between and all other prepositions are followed by the objective case:

- He stood before you and me
- The truth is within you and me
- The sky is above you and him (not he)

So between you and me, this isn't all that hard, is it?

> *Tip for Fiction Writers:* To keep from cluttering up your prose when writing a short flashback, only use the past perfect tense (had) in the first and last sentences of that section. This will signal to the reader when you start talking about something that occurred in the past and when that reflection ends. Take all those other "hads" out and you'll have a much cleaner read.

I'M ONTO YOU

I sometimes have trouble with the preposition *onto*. Some of the time it's pretty easy to know when I mean *on to* (two words), but other times I'm not so sure. This is how most dictionaries or grammar guides will explain it:

- If you can precede *onto* with the word *up*, then it's one word: The dog jumped onto the table.

That's pretty clear. It implies a positioning on something. Here are some instances where you want two words:

- Hold on to my arm.
- Get on to the next part, please.
- Let's move on to better things.
- Please hold on to this bag for me

But you do say:

- Hook the wire onto the nail
- They're onto us [colloquialism].

Into is a lot easier, but writers still mess it up. We say: take into account, go into teaching, get into trouble, late into the night, run into a wall, look up into the sky.

But you don't want to "turn yourself *into* the police" because that would require a cool magic trick to transform yourself like that.

And you don't give *into* my demands because to "give in" is a verb-preposition combo structure. Just like you don't fall *into* line. You "fall in" to line.

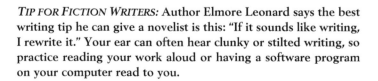

> *TIP FOR FICTION WRITERS:* Author Elmore Leonard says the best writing tip he can give a novelist is this: "If it sounds like writing, I rewrite it." Your ear can often hear clunky or stilted writing, so practice reading your work aloud or having a software program on your computer read to you.

ARE YOU BETWEEN OR AMONG?

What's a little joke between friends? Assuming there are just two of you, *between* is correct. But if you're talking about a larger circle of friends, you'll want to use *among*.

Often people think *between* is used only when referring to two persons, objects, or groups. It's true that when the choice is between two distinct options, *between* is the right choice.

- Edith couldn't decide between the red or black dress.
- Jeremy's college choice was between Harvard and Yale.

But *between* is also correct when there are more than two options. CMOS explains it this way: Between is "perfectly appropriate for more than two objects if multiple one-to-one relationships are understood from the context."

For example:

- Among the Christmas dresses on the sale rack, Edith's final choice was between a red sequined dress and a black velvet gown.

Even though Edith has more than two options, her decision has come down to one of two.

Or this example:

- The tensions between the board, faculty, and students were on edge following the Halloween prank.

But if you were to refer a group as a whole, *among* would be the word to use:

- Tensions among the students ran at fever pitch.

Among can also refer to a relationship within a group.

- Among the members of his caucus, Roberts was considered the most conservative.
- Rosie was ill at ease among the members of the country club.

Between and *among* also function as location or direction words. Here their meanings lend specificity to a sentence.

- Joe found the treasure between the trees. (Implies only two trees)
- Joe found the treasure among the trees. (Multiple trees)
- Martha walked between her classmates. (They walked three abreast; implies moving in a specific direction)
- Martha walked among her classmates. (Implies a casual scene of mingling, not moving in a defined direction or with purpose)

EITHER OR, NEITHER NOR

It doesn't matter if you pronounce *either* with a long e (ēther) or a long i (īther). Depending on your region of the country, one may be preferred, but either pronunciation is correct. However, it is important that you know when and how to use these words and their partners *or* and *nor* correctly.

Either and *neither* are comparison words. They are used to compare two alternatives or options—not more.

- When John met with the dean he was told, "Either apply yourself to your studies or drop out of college." (The dean might have given John more than two options, but if he did, he wouldn't use *either*.)
- The dean told John to pick one of the following options: apply himself to his studies, hire a tutor, or drop out of school. (*Either* would not be correct in this instance.)

Either is always paired with or; neither is always paired with nor. Use either-*or* to compare two possibilities.

- We can either eat before the movie or afterward.

Use *neither-nor* to compare things that are not true.

- Neither students nor their professors were alerted to the early dismissal.

It's possible to state the negative in another way:

- The administration did not alert either the students or their professors to the early dismissal.

Notice that *neither-nor* becomes *either-or* in that case because you wouldn't want to use a double negative.

Nor can be used without *neither* if it is the continuation of a negative thought. In the following example it functions as *and not* or *or not*.

- I do not speak French. Nor do I know Greek.

MORE RULES FOR EITHER OR, NEITHER NOR

Here's something else to keep in mind when you use either-or or neither-nor. If both alternatives are singular, use a singular verb.

- Either Mary or Jane will make the favors for the party. (*Mary* and *Jane* are both singular, so the verb is singular.)
- Neither the bride nor the groom was at the church on time. (*Bride* and *groom* are each singular; use a singular verb.)

But if one of the subjects is plural, use a plural verb.

- Either Mary or the bridesmaids are going to make the wedding favors. (*Bridesmaids* is plural; use a plural verb.)
- Neither the groom nor his parents were invited to the bridal shower. (*Parents* is plural, so the plural verb *were* is correct.)

And finally, pay close attention to the placement of either. In the following example, both things are wanted, so *either* comes after the verb:

- Wrong: He either wanted to go to Hawaii or Europe on their honeymoon.
- Correct: He wanted to go to either Hawaii or Europe on their honeymoon.

If, however, the action (look at the verb) is different in regard to the things being compared, it is correct for *either* to come before the verb.

- He either earned a promotion before the wedding or found another way to pay off his car.

TIP FOR FICTION WRITERS: Using the word **as** often weakens a sentence. For example, instead of writing "As I opened the door, I reached for my keys," change to "I opened the door and reached for my keys." If it's not crucial to show one thing happening **as** another happens, it may be better to take **as** out.

WHILE MEANS WHEREAS . . . SOMETIMES

We usually think of *while* to mean "during the time that," but it can be used to mean "whereas." This can create a problem in meaning—which depends solely upon the use of a small bit of punctuation.

In the first example below, *while* is not preceded by a comma. In the second example, *while* must be preceded by a comma.

- I can't talk on the phone while my little sister is screaming.
- The Pacific Ocean is often calm, while the Atlantic Ocean is rough.

The use or omission of the comma may not seem like a big deal, but if you write "The Pacific Ocean is often calm while the Atlantic Ocean is rough," the meaning is entirely different. In this sentence you are saying that one ocean is calm *at the same time* that the other is rough. Which is nothing like saying one ocean is calm *in contrast to* the other ocean.

Some purists and copyeditors tend to frown on the use of *while* to mean *whereas* because the meaning depends so heavily upon the comma, and points of punctuation have a habit of not being where they should be. But that seems a silly argument—since so much meaning is often clarified or defined by a single bit of punctuation.

Those "little bits" have big roles to play in language, but it's true writers often ignore them, perhaps thinking their "size" relates to their importance. But don't succumb to that erroneous belief! Pay attention to your little bits.

If you choose to use *while* to mean *whereas*, it's important to remember that comma!

> *TIP FOR FICTION WRITERS:* **Listen to this fiction-writing advice from author Kurt Vonnegut: "Give the reader at least one character he or she can root for. Every character should want something, even if it is only a glass of water. Every sentence must do one of two things—reveal character or advance the action. Start as close to the end as possible." I personally feel these bits of advice are some of the best a writer can heed.**

NOTES

NOTES

OTHER RULES OF GRAMMAR

DO YOU KNOW WHEN TO USE (THOSE) PARENTHESES?

Parentheses sometimes confuse writers. When you want to put something in parentheses within a sentence, the ending punctuation goes outside the parentheses for that entire sentence. Example:

- I went to the store (but I didn't buy anything).
- With a separate thought enclosed in parentheses, the punctuation goes inside. Example:
- I went to the store. (Really, I didn't buy anything!)

Want to get a little more complex? If you have two complete sentences inside parentheses, only the first sentence gets terminal punctuation:

- The instructions (Place tab A in the slot. Leave tab B alone) were confusing.

If you are using a list of sorts in a sentences and you have something in parentheses, put the comma after the parentheses. Example:

- I bought eggs, celery (which was a little wilted), and crackers.

I hope (for everyone's sake) that my explanation makes sense!

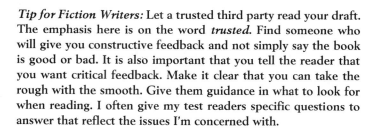

> *Tip for Fiction Writers:* Let a trusted third party read your draft. The emphasis here is on the word *trusted.* Find someone who will give you constructive feedback and not simply say the book is good or bad. It is also important that you tell the reader that you want critical feedback. Make it clear that you can take the rough with the smooth. Give them guidance in what to look for when reading. I often give my test readers specific questions to answer that reflect the issues I'm concerned with.

SOME GRAMMATICAL ERRORS THAT AREN'T

Don't you love all the rules we have for grammar? One thing you learn early on in elementary school is that for every rule, there is an exception— or two or three. All you have to do is say aloud these words that seem as if they should be pronounced the same: cough, though, through, enough, trough, tough, and though. That just about sums up the silliness and inconsistencies of the English language.

With that said, here are a few "rules" that are no longer rules. Yes, you have permission to break them. Times have changed. If enough people ignore the rules, after a while they won't be observed any more. Or something like that.

- *Never split an infinitive.* Meaning you are supposed to keep the "to" with the infinitive form of the verb. The famous example of rule-breaking is the line from the opening of the old *Star Trek* show: "To boldly go where no man has gone before." The rule would require it to be rewritten to "to go boldly." But does it matter? No. So feel free to blatantly ignore [I just did right here--do you see?] the rule.

- *Never end a sentence with a preposition.* Go ahead. I mean, seriously— what rule book is this from? What's it leading to? Isn't this something we can just get through? See, there's nothing wrong with ending a sentence with a preposition. I always like the funny way of making this point: "A preposition is something you should never end a sentence with." 'Nuff said.

- *Never begin a sentence with a conjunction.* In case you don't recall what those are, think of the acronym FANBOYS: for, and, nor, but, or, yet, so. So feel free to use them to start a sentence. But don't do it all the time. Or your writing will sound a bit choppy. Or not. So what?

Got any rules you like to break in your writing? I'll bet you're not the only one.

BECAUSE OF OR DUE TO CONFUSION

Let me take this opportunity to confuse you a bit. Maybe you're already confused about some things. I'm often confused. Thankfully, there are lots of great resources available to "unconfuse" me.

Here are two phrases that often muddle writers: *Due to* and *because of*. Is there a difference and does it matter?

The phrase *due to* accompanies nouns:

- "Her bad grade was due to her failure to study." (Bad grade=noun.)
- The phrase *because of* accompanies verbs:
- "She failed because of not studying." (Failed=verb.)

Sure, you can say "She failed due to a lack of studying." But it's traditionally correct to follow this rule, and that example is a bit clunky. Why not just say, "She failed because she didn't study"? That works too.

> *Tip for Fiction Writers:* Use bargain words instead of fancy ones. Don't try to bolster a sentence by cluttering it up. There are few things that scream "amateur" or "pretentious" more than trying to impress a reader with an unusual, unknown word. The phrase I remember is "Don't use a five-dollar word when a good five-cent word will do." I always tell my editing clients "less is more." Often fewer, concise words will pack a bigger punch than a sentence with a long list of flowery adjectives.

> *TIP FOR FICTION WRITERS:* Redundancy plagues all writers at times. We may write without thinking phrases such as "blue in color," "larger in size," "twelve in number," "handsome in appearance," and "square in shape." Keep your eye open for such redundancies and cull them out.

ABBREVIATED DETAILS

We writers occasionally use abbreviations in our writing, so there are a few fairly intuitive rules that apply to these shortened word forms.

First, when should you use an article (such as *the* or *an*) before an abbreviated term or name? Generally, if "the" is part of the name but not absorbed by the abbreviation, use "the" as if the abbreviation were spelled out. Here are some examples *The Chicago Manual of Style* gives:

- The NFL comprises thirty-two teams.
- NFL games rarely get postponed owing to inclement weather.
- In its ninety-two years, the NAACP has been a cornerstone of American civil liberties organizations.
- NAACP membership is open to all who can afford it.
- Advertisers for AT&T made a splash by incorporating the wah-wah pedal into recent advertisements for high-bandwidth cable.
- Do you listen to the BBC?

What about putting the letter *a* in front of an acronym? Would you write "A NFL game doesn't interest me"?

We're taught you only use *an* if the article precedes a vowel. However, writers should write what they say. Acronyms are called initialisms, which means they are constructs of initials. You would say literally "En Ef El," so, as is the rule with words that follow the articles *a* and *an*, anything that begins with a vowel *sound* should be treated as if starting with a vowel.

I will gladly give you *an* MBA in grammar for writing "*an* NFL game."

> TIP FOR FICTION WRITERS: "I know too many people who've spent months working over the first chapters of their projected novels. That's wrong. Get it down. Bumble it through. Tell the story. When you have fifty or a hundred pages typed, you've got something to work with." ~ Mary Higgins Clark

WALK TOWARD, NOT TOWARDS

In US English, you usually leave off the *s* on directional terms like toward, forward, and backward. Even though we may speak that way, it's not correct grammar in writing. The exception is in the accepted usage of *backwards*, according to Bryan Garner.

Here's what he says in *Garner's Modern American Usage*: "An exception in AmE is the adverb *backwards*, which is used frequently (though still much less often than *backward*) . . . When *backward* and *forward* combine in a phrase, be consistent about using the *s*." He says leaving the *s* off is more common. As an adjective, *backward* is acceptable: "It was a backward move."

- Wrong: "He walked towards the building."
- Correct: "He walked toward the building."
- Wrong: "The car rocked backwards and forwards."
- Correct: "The car rocked backward and forward."

Here are some words in American English that do best without the *s* at the end: *downward, outward, seaward, rearward, skyward, toward, upward*.

There's also little difference between words like *southern* and *southerly*: "The bees escaped and moved northward" or "They moved in a northerly fashion." However, Garner emphasizes that sometimes you don't need to add the word *direction*, since it's a bit redundant and cumbersome:

- Clunky: "Turn down High Street and head in a northerly direction." Better: "Turn down High Street and head north."

TIP FOR FICTION WRITERS: C. S. Lewis wrote: "The reader, we must remember, does not start by knowing what we mean. If our words are ambiguous, our meaning will escape him. . . . I sometimes think that writing is like driving sheep down a road. If there is any gate open to the left or the right the reader will most certainly go into it." Watch those gates and make sure they're latched.

ARE YOU DIFFERENT FROM OR DIFFERENT THAN?

Comparisons. We live in a world in which we are often called upon to make comparisons. Does WalMart or Target have the better price on something? Is Brad Pitt a better actor than Paul Rudd? Are you comparing these *with* or *to* each other?

It seems like a small distinction, but most writers' guides agree that if you are noting the similarities between two things, *comparing to* is the correct terminology. If you're pointing out differences, you use *compared with*.

- Robert compared Barnes and Nobles's prices to Amazon's. (comparing similar things)
- Australia is in a good economic position compared with many other countries. (comparing one country with another)

Speaking of differences, is there a difference between *different from* and *different than*? A slight one, most grammarians agree, though for much of history they have been used interchangeably. *Different from* means "not the same." Use it to convey contrast.

- This outfit is different from the one I ordered.
- Alex's perspective on the economy is different from George's.

Different is an adjective; *different from* should be followed by a noun, pronoun, or phrase.

Than implies a comparison and is used with a comparison adjective, such as more, less, better, colder, prettier, etc.

- My sister's home is bigger than mine, but she still refuses to host the family gathering.

Than also functions as a conjunction,   and you may remember that conjunctions join clauses. So different than is the right choice when it's followed by a clause.

- Peter's freshman year of college was much different than he expected.

Differently is an adverb and takes the comparison than when used in the adverbial phrase *differently than*.

- My mother views the world differently than I do.

We may have differences of opinion, but I hope we can agree that my opinion, although different from yours, is still valid.

KEEPING UP WITH THE JONESES

Apostrophes seem to give people a hard time. I'm not sure why. I have to restrain myself when I see (which is often) an incorrect use of apostrophes on restaurant signs and in menus. Why they are so common there, I'm not sure, but it's a good thing for all writers to memorize these rules—and they're not hard.

What is wrong with the sentences below?

- He was selling chocolates to the participant's.
- The Milky Way's were a better choice.
- Vast majority of people have TV's .
- They were a well-known group in the 1960's.

Answer: The apostrophe is incorrectly used in place of a plural. It should be participants, Ways, TVs, and 1960s.

There are two uses for the apostrophe—in shortened forms, indicating a verb added after the apostrophe (it's, couldn't) and in possessives (It's George's house).

What should we do when a possessive is also a plural?

- My sisters' room is messy. (Means more than one. If you only have one sister, it's just *sister's*.)
- My parents' house is close by. (If you mean only one parent, it would be "my parent's house.")

Another big error I see is in pluralizing single names and other nouns that end with *s*. Yes, it does look a bit funny, but these are correct:

- Robert Burns's poetry
- Jesus's sermons
- The waitress's uniform; the genius's brain
- And here's the tricky one:
- The Joneses' house (meaning a house belonging to more than one Jones—a couple or family, for example. Remember the expression: "Keeping up with the Joneses." And because "Joneses" is plural, not singular, you just use the apostrophe, like "the Smiths' house.")
- James's family but The Jameses (the whole family). And again, the Jameses' house.

I hope this will help you stay out of trouble with the Grammar Joneses!

DON'T "TRY AND" DO ANYTHING

One of my big pet peeves is the "try and" construction, which many writers fall victim to because we have learned to talk this way. I see this often in published novels; obviously, the copyeditors and proofreaders of many publishing houses don't catch this error either.

When you use this phrase you are not talking about both trying *and* doing something else. You are talking about trying *to* do something.

Wrong:

- Try *and* help me move this boulder.
- I want to try *and* understand what you are saying.
- Correct:
- Try *to* help me move this boulder.
- I want to try *to* understand what you are saying.
- Try *to* pay attention to this often misused expression.

This also applies to the phrase "be sure and . . ."—as in "be sure and tell him I'm coming." The correct way to say this is "be sure to tell him I'm coming."

Tip for Fiction Writers: After you get feedback from test readers, keep in mind that big issues need to be considered carefully. Sometimes a reader will not like a section or suggest changes that go beyond simple sentence structure. In these cases you need to consider the feedback carefully and only make changes that you feel improve the book. It's your book, and if you listen to everyone else's advice, it can sometimes make your book worse, not better.

COULDA, WOULDA, SHOULDA

"Coulda, woulda, shoulda" goes the regretful refrain made popular by a song of the same name.

It's the lament any of us might utter when we realize we've made a poor choice or followed a path that didn't end up where we'd hoped it would.

I hope you also share my regret over the abuse of this phrase—this rendering being an even more egregious error than the one sometimes seen in print: could of, would of, should of. That may be what you hear, but what someone is really saying is *have*, not *of*.

- I could have taken you to the airport if you would have let me know.

When we're speaking, we tend to run our words together and form the contraction *could've*. But what we hear is this:

- I could of taken you to the airport if you would of let me know.

What's so awful about that construction? *Could, would, should* are members of the verb family. Technically, they are auxiliary or helping verbs. Because they are "assisting" verbs, they always occur in a phrase—which consists of other verbs. In this example, *could have taken* is a verb phrase. (For the record, *of* is not a verb, so it cannot be part of a verb phrase.)

People who insist on writing *could of* (or *would of* or *should of*) ought to receive thirty lashes with a wet noodle.

TIP FOR FICTION WRITERS: The simplest way to make dialog less formal or stilted is to use more contractions. Unless a character is the type that speaks that way due to status or nationality, think about changing "I am" to "I'm" and "I cannot" to "I can't." You use contractions, so your characters should too.

SOME INCORRECT CONSTRUCTIONS TO AVOID

Here are some phrases or sentence constructions I come across often in my editing. Although they're common, it's good to pay attention to these expressions and make sure they make sense. We should strive to make sense in our writing, right?

- "I don't know whether I should go to the movies." Whether or what?
- "He took a different way home." Different from what?
- "It's a quality paper." What kind of quality? Bad or good?

When using a word that calls for comparing one thing to another, you need to make clear what those two things are.

Here's another common expression: "I could care less." What in the world does that mean? Nothing, really. The correct expression is "I couldn't care less." Which means you care very little about something. That's an expression that makes a point.

But it's also a cliché, and you want to avoid clichés unless it fits in with a character's personality and POV. But maybe you couldn't care less.

TIP FOR FICTION WRITERS: Although grammarians have agreed for hundreds of years that using *like* as a conjunction is not standard grammar, even *The Chicago Manual of Style* acknowledges that it is increasingly acceptable in spoken and colloquial usage and advises "consider context and tone when deciding whether to impose standard English."

ARE YOU IN THE SUBJUNCTIVE MOOD?

I'm going to spend a few entries on what I think is an interesting and sometimes confusing component of our language: the subjunctive mood.

Contrary to what some say, the subjunctive is not a tense; it's a mood. *Tense* refers to *when* an action takes place (past, present, future), while mood merely reflects *how* the speaker feels about the action. When deciding whether to use this "mood" or not, a writer needs to stop and think about the intent in the sentence she wants to write. I often see the subjunctive used incorrectly, or not used when it should be.

The subjunctive mood is rarely used in English, but it is widely used in Spanish and other languages. Subjunctive forms of verbs are typically used to express various states of unreality such as wish, emotion, possibility, judgment, opinion, necessity, or action that has not yet occurred.

Let's start with a simple comparison. English verbs have three moods: indicative, imperative, and subjunctive.

- I will go to sleep now. Do you want to go to sleep now? (Indicative mood: used to state a fact or opinion or ask a question)
- Go to sleep now! Please, go to sleep now. (Imperative mood: expresses a command, gives a direction, or makes a request)
- If I were you, I would go to sleep now. (Subjunctive mood: expresses wishes, suggestions, and other attitudes)

Forming the subjunctive mood in present tense is very simple—use the base form of the verb *regardless of the subject.*

- My teacher insisted that *I study* harder.

Here's the tricky part—just when do you use the subjunctive? You want to use it with contrary-to-fact clauses that state imaginary or hypothetical conditions (often called conditional statements). Such statements usually begin with *if* (or *unless*) or follow the verb *wish.*

For present contrary-to-fact clauses, use the verb's past tense; if the verb is *to be*, use *were.*

- If I were rich and had a yacht, I would cruise all over the world.
- I wish I were wise and beautiful, but I am stupid and ugly.

I hope this first lesson has been easy to understand. If I were brilliant, I would have explained this better.

ANOTHER LOOK AT THE SUBJUNCTIVE MOOD

Let's take a further look into the subjunctive mood, since there are often places in our writing where this "mood" is just what we need. The thing to remember about using the subjunctive structure is that it is used for imaginary or hypothetical conditions. Think for a moment about the difference between these sentences:

- If I was home, I would have caught the intruder.
- If I were home, I would have caught the intruder.
- If I had been home, I would have caught the intruder.

In the first example, it's assumed the statement could possibly have been true; it's not an imaginary or hypothetical situation. If, in truth, I was home at the time, I would have caught that intruder.

In the second example, the subjunctive signals the reader that this situation is only hypothetical. It implies: I wish I had been home, for if I had been, I would have caught that bad guy.

The third sentence is again a realistic possibility. It isn't a wish. I'm stating that yes, if I had been home, I would have caught the intruder.

So take a moment to understand the subjunctive mood; if it were in my power, I'd make this easier for you.

TIP FOR FICTION WRITERS: **When editing and revising your work, look for one type of problem at a time. Read through your text several times, concentrating first on sentence structures, then word choice, then spelling, and finally punctuation. As the saying goes: If you look for trouble, you're likely to find it.**

TIP FOR FICTION WRITERS: **Increase your vocabulary by looking up words you come across that you don't know, then jot them in a notebook or in the Notes sections in this book. Don't learn obscure words just to impress readers. However, there may be instances that call for an unusual or uncommon word. If you learn new words for the purpose of enriching your knowledge of English, you will find that in time your writing will deepen.**

HOW TO DECIDE IF YOU SHOULD USE THE SUBJUNCTIVE MOOD

When I'm unclear whether to use the subjunctive or not, I replace the subjunctive verb form with the normal indicative. For example, I might write:

- If I were home, I would catch that intruder.

I then rewrite it this way, in past tense, and if it could be a true possibility in my scene, I know I should not use the subjunctive:

- If I had been home, I would have caught that intruder.

Hmm, that is a true, not hypothetical, statement, so this is the correct way to write that line:

- "If I was home, I would catch that intruder."

We also use present subjunctive in statements that express a suggestion, requirement, or request. Such statements use verbs such as ask, insist, urge, require, demand, recommend, and suggest. These verbs often precede a subordinate clause beginning with *that*, with the clause containing the substance of the request, requirement, or suggestion.

- The doctor insisted that *she walk* at least a mile a day.
- The professor requires that *each student write* six essays in the course.
- John's father demanded that *he apologize* for burning down the neighbors' house.

Auxiliary verbs *could, would,* and *should* might also express the subjunctive mood, especially when one expresses a condition contrary to fact.

- If the forecast were correct, I would be prepared. (Condition contrary to fact: If the forecast could be correct, I would be prepared.)
- If Bill were to marry Sally, he would be happy. (Condition contrary to fact: If Bill should marry Sally, he would be happy.)

You probably had no idea there was so much to the subjunctive mood. If I were to list all the ways you could use this mood, this entry would be very long!

NEGATIVE, CONTINUOUS, AND PASSIVE FORMS OF SUBJUNCTIVE MOOD

The subjunctive mood is one we often use without thinking. But often writers use it incorrectly in writing, so it is worthwhile to take a close look at this interesting "mood" we use all the time. This structure is used not only for positive statements but also with negative, continuous, and passive constructs.

Negative Examples:

- The boss insisted that John not be at the meeting.
- The company asked that employees not accept personal phone calls during business hours.
- I suggest that you not take the job without renegotiating the salary.

Passive Examples:

- Matt recommended that Debbie be hired immediately.
- Lee demanded that I be allowed to take part in the negotiations.
- We suggested that you be admitted to the organization.

Continuous Examples:

- It is important that you be standing there when he gets off the plane.
- It is crucial that a car be waiting for the boss when the meeting is over.
- I propose that we all be waiting in Tim's apartment when he gets home.

These forms of the subjunctive have nothing to do with hypothetical or wishful situations, which is what many writers associate with the subjunctive mood. However, sometimes this use of the subjunctive can sound stiff and formal. If that's not the tone and style you want in your writing or in your characters' POVs, you might want to ditch the subjunctive.

- When he gets off the plane, you better be standing there.
- Make sure a car is waiting for the boss after the meeting.
- I propose we all wait in Tim's apartment until he gets home.

Sometimes these differences are subtle, so it behooves writers to take a moment to think through the specific meaning they want to convey in a sentence. It is important that you be mindful of how you write!

DO SIGNS READ?

Do you find it a little kooky (I do) that we have expressions like "the sign said . . ." or "the notice read . . ."? I mean, signs can't talk, and notices haven't gone to school. But what's implied by these expressions is something along the lines of "the person who wrote the sign said . . ."

Regardless, since signs aren't people or talking animals, they don't need speaker tags. If you remember the rule, whenever you use a speaker tag, you put a comma before the speech: George said, "Keep out."

With something like a sign you don't need the comma. Just say: The sign said "Keep Out."

If you are referring to a type of sign or notice, just give it initial caps.

- Pay attention to the No Smoking sign
- I ignored the Keep Out sign

The same principle applies to forms:

- Fill out that Consent to Search form

In your spare time, if you're bored, you could try to teach your signs to read. Good luck.

> *TIP FOR FICTION WRITERS:* **When going through a draft of your writing, consider reviewing a hard copy (if you don't mind wasting paper). Print out your document and review it line by line. Rereading your work in a different format may help you catch errors that you previously missed. To save paper, single space your text and reduce the font size one point. Go for two-sided printing. If you read pages in random order, too, you can catch mistakes better.**

MESSY PLURALS

Plurals can get messy. and the rules even messier. The Chicago Manual of Style tends toward logic, but in certain cases meaning can still be a bit obscure, and rewriting might be the best choice for a writer facing sentences like these:

- All the listeners followed the beat in their hearts. [plural "hearts," since they don't all share one heart]
- The children put their hats on their heads. [The children don't share one head, yet *Chicago* says, "Please note, however, that people don't always talk that way; the construction that omits the *s* is common and accepted in many contexts.]
- I used 1 1/2 cups of sugar [although you'd think "one cup" is singular].
- He had .5 percentage points and zero dollars. [Okay, is that counterintuitive to you too?]

The most common mistake I see when editing is the addition of apostrophes to plurals. It's so widespread everywhere, in fact, that I'm beginning to believe it's an epidemic. All these apostrophes for plurals below are *wrong*:

- I saw three B-52's flying overhead.
- Everyone, show your ID's.
- I have six cool CD's and five DVD's.

To avoid confusion, though, there are times when you need an apostrophe for a plural, such as with "getting all A's" (so the word doesn't look like as) and with lowercase terms like abc's or p's and q's.

> *TIP FOR FICTION WRITERS:* Create your own proofreading checklist. Keep a list of the mistakes you commonly make, then refer to that list each time you proofread. Write down words you often use incorrectly. By doing this you can't help but become a better self-editor.

EACH WRITER SHOULD CORRECT THEIR OWN GRAMMAR

Dreading to deal with the ubiquitous "their," let's just get it over with. It's become so common for us to say things like "Do you know someone who lives alone and worries for their life?" or "Everyone in the audience blew their nose." How about "No one knew what their assignment was"? And so on.

We have gotten into the habit of using "their" as a catch-all word in sentences that really call for a singular pronoun. And often the best way around these glaring pitfalls is to rewrite.

It is clunky to say "his" or "her": "Each person in the room scratched his or her head."

But although it's easier to defer to "Each person scratched their head," why not rewrite this so it's a stronger sentence? Or if it the information is not necessary, just take it out. Do you really need to tell the reader that everyone scratched their head? Just what are you trying to say?

If you are referring to a group of people or objects or animals, using "their" will depend on the emphasis you are aiming for. If you say "The audience is listening" (heard that slogan before?), the "audience" is being treated as a singular noun or entity. If you say "The couple are having marital problems," you are implying that both in the relationship as individuals

are having difficulty with their marriage. You can also say "The couple is having trouble" if you want to make them a singular entity, but the emphasis is slightly different.

Just know that some pronouns are only singular: each, either, everybody, everyone, everything, neither, nobody, nothing, somebody, someone, something. When you construct a sentence with these, the verb needs to be singular: "Each is responsible for his own book."

Sorry, no "their" allowed.

And so as not to confuse you further, I won't tell you about the pronouns that can be either singular or plural. I'll plague you with that in another entry.

LET'S BE IN AGREEMENT

I think we can all agree that subjects and verbs need to agree with one another. A singular subject takes a singular verb.

- Nancy is the school librarian.

Plural subjects take plural verbs:

- Nancy and Ned are friends.

But we don't always write with such simple subjects. What is the correct verb form in these sentences?

- A pack of wolves was/were howling in the distance.
- A bundle of ballots was/were found in the official's car.
- A flock of geese is/are migrating overhead.

Each subject includes both a singular and a plural noun: pack—singular/wolves—plural; bundle—singular/ballots—plural; flock—singular/geese—plural. So do you use a singular or plural verb?

I could get into a lot of technical terms here like *notional* vs. *formal agreement* and *predeterminer*. But I prefer *Merriam-Webster's* "plain sense" solution: "When you have a collecting noun phrase (*a bunch of*) before a plural noun (*the boys*), the sense will normally be plural and so should the verb."

But there is another way of understanding this. A noun/subject phrase like "a bundle of ballots" includes a head noun—bundle. The noun establishes whether the verb is singular or plural. In most cases, that will be correct.

Applying this principle to the above examples, we would choose the following verbs:

- A pack of wolves was howling . . . (The intent or emphasis here is on the pack—singular.)
- A bundle of ballots was found . . . (One item—bundle—was located someplace.)
- A flock of geese is migrating . . . (Though, it would not be improper to say a flock of geese *are* migrating, if your emphasis is on the geese themselves rather than the flock.)

Don't you love it when you get to determine what's right and wrong, for a change?

MORE DANGLING THINGS

Here are some more dangling things. These are called dangling (and misplaced) modifiers. A writer might start a sentence with a modifying phrase, but all too often she doesn't start the second phrase with the correct noun (that goes with it). Here are some examples of misplaced modifiers:

- With one hundred years of experience, you can count on Sears. [You don't have a hundred years of experience.]
- As a scientist, his lab is far from his home. [His lab is not a scientist.]
- Fresh out of school, finding a job was impossible. ["Finding a job" is not fresh out of school.]
- Doctors see babies once they finish their residency. [Do babies go through residency?]
- They visited the lions at the zoo after they ate a zebra. [Who ate the zebra?]
- They are writing a newsletter for parents of teens who take drugs. [Are the parents or the teens taking the drugs?]
- This is a novel of betrayal by a famous author. [Did the author betray someone?]
- She followed the man into the store with determination. [Never knew a store could be so determined!]

These are easy to fix, of course, just by rewording. If you look for sentences you write that have two nouns (subject and object) in them that will help you spot the potential problem.

TIP FOR FICTION WRITERS: Italics are used in fiction for emphasis, but like any good thing, if you use them too often, they will not only be hard to read but will weaken the emphasis desired. Used sparingly, they can hit home with a word or phrase. But be careful not to rely on italicizing to make the reader pay attention to what is important. Try to have the wording, word choice, and show of emotion by the character put the emphasis on the bit of speech that needs to stand out.

DON'T DANGLE

I see a lot of dangling participles. Okay, you are probably wondering just what the darn things are (so you can avoid them)! Here are some examples:

- While writing the memo, the phone rang [the phone is writing the memo]
- Having been told she was always late, an alarm clock was the solution [the clock was told it was late, and it's a girl clock!]
- Upon opening the door, the handle was stuck [the handle is opening the door]
- When writing a sentence, the pen slipped. [the pen is writing the sentence]
- While racing up the hill, my tears gushed out [the tears are racing up the hill]
- Driving down the street, the mansion came into view [the mansion is driving]

These types of things are called "dangling" because the participial phrase seems to hang in the air unattached to any subject. So always be sure to match the initial action taking place with the correct subject:

- While I was writing the memo, the phone rang, or
- While writing the memo, I heard the phone ring.

These may be a bit tricky to spot, but be alert to those sentences in which you start with a dependent phrase (incomplete) using a gerund (a word with *ing*). I prefer in my own writing to rewrite the sentence so that I don't start with an incomplete phrase. I feel my writing comes across cleaner that way.

TIP FOR FICTION WRITERS: **"Pushing yourself physically prepares you to work hard mentally." Vonnegut did pushups as a break from writing. Murakami runs ten kilometers each day. A. J. Jacobs types while walking on a treadmill. You can decide what works for you, but make sure you get out and move. Exercise can also help clear the clutter from your head and shake off your sleepiness in the afternoon.**

EACH THING MUST BE THE SAME

Do you remember the old Sesame Street shows? I grew up singing that song that asks "which of these things doesn't belong?" When you are listing a number of things in sequence in a sentence, be careful of faulty parallelism. I see this a lot. If you "list" three things in parallel construction, make sure each element is the same kind. Sometimes "one of these things just doesn't belong."

Wrong:

• I ate potatoes, apples, then dug in the garden.

Correct:

• She ate potatoes, ate apples, then dug in the garden.
• She ate potatoes and apples, then went outside and dug in the garden. (You need a verb to go along with each object.)

The way to check your parallelism is to restate the sentence with the first part of the phrase matching each part: "She ate potatoes. She ate apples. She dug in the garden." The word *she* starts each phrase.

Wrong:

• She likes singing, dancing, and to play the violin.

Correct:

• She likes singing, dancing, and playing the violin. (Each word in the sentence has to be in the same form.
Another way you could rewrite that would be "She likes to sing, dance, and play the violin," as the word *to* goes correctly with each verb.)

Wrong:

• I like to eat chocolate, playing card games, and riddles.

Correct:

• I like to eat chocolate, play card games, and tell riddles.

Watch to make sure, as in the above example, that the verb forms are the same in all the items in your list. This would also be correct:

• I like to eating chocolate, playing card games, and telling riddles.

SHARE AND SHARE ALIKE

Would you say "This is Joe's and Sally's car" or "This is Joe and Sally's car"? This type of question can come up a lot in writing. The rule is that you only need the apostrophe + *s* after the second name if the two people share the item noted.

- John and Mary's marriage is on the rocks.
- Bill and Nina's escrow closed last week.
- Mike and John's team won the division.

So, conversely, if two people do not share the item or issue in question, you would need them each to have the apostrophe + *s*.

- Both Frank's and Sara's job contracts will get renewed.
- Bob's and Ted's adventures went well [no, this isn't about their joint excellent adventure].

The same idea applies to words that are plural:

- The doctors' and the lawyers' conventions went well [two different conventions].
- The actors and actresses' show went well [they were in the same show].

Don't get me started, though, about how I feel when I hear "Hey, mine and you guys's car is the same!" Sadly, I hear that kind of sentence structure a lot!

TIP FOR FICTION WRITERS: **There are no CMOS rules for how internal thoughts should be expressed in fiction writing. Most writers use italics to show a character thinking a direct thought. But other writers, such as Orson Scott Card, run the internal thinking alongside narrative without changing the font style. Whatever method you choose, just make sure it's clear the character is thinking these thoughts. If you don't, it could confuse your reader.**

ACRONYMS AND PERIODS

Back in the day, it seemed we put periods in every acronym. Much of that has changed from when I was in elementary school. That was way before zip codes and two-letter state abbreviations. That was even before calculators, copy machines, and yes, even area codes. But I'm not here to talk about my age (by now you're imagining I'm about ninety).

So, in case you don't know what an acronym is, I could give you the long, tedious definition in *Merriam-Webster's*, but I'll spare you and just say that if you take the first letter of each word in a name or phrase and put them together, you have an acronym. They're everywhere, and just about every corporation seems to have one.

Here are a few: IBM, NATO, FAFSA, LASER . . . and now we have chat and Internet acronyms like LOL and BFF, BFN, BRB (I always thought that meant "bathroom break," but that could apply, right?), DBEYR and FWIW (okay, if you're not up on all these, don't concern yourself).

In this fast-food fast world, we seem to want to shorten everything we say and write. Maybe someday everything will have been converted to acronyms. I can picture it now. Well, if you watch your kids text, they are already doing it. Maybe it makes you ROFL, but I often shake my head confused.

So, getting BOT (back on topic), the rule for using periods with acronyms is pretty simple.

- Leave periods out for acronyms with capital letters, even if they have lowercase letters in there somewhere: US, UN, PhD, NY, IL, and so on.

Abbreviations have some differences, so if you are using an abbreviation that uses lowercase letters, you normally keep the period in.

- a.m., p.m., i.e., etc., etc. [*Chicago* lists a.k.a. but *Webster's* uses aka. I prefer the latter, since simpler and shorter is better to me.]
- If you're writing a name with initials for the first and middle names, you'd use periods, such as in my name, C. S. Lakin [there is always a space between the first two initials but not when using three initials, like G.R.R. Martin].
- However, you would use just letters when a complete name has been changed into initials, like JFK.

Should you ever spell out an acronym? If you're not too sure the term is universally understood, and you plan to refer to it numerous times in your writing, yes, spell it out the first time, and after that just use the acronym. A good way to do that is to use the acronym, then spell it out in parentheses following.

MIND OTHER PEOPLE'S BUSINESS

What's a writer to do when she needs to make a normally plural word possessive? Words like others, people, children, and women can muddy up the grammatical waters sometimes. I often see writers adding the possessive apostrophe + *s* in the oddest places. But I get the confusion. Let's see if we can simplify this.

If you are talking about one person, you would write this:

- It's not my opinion but the other's opinion.
- It's that person's car, not mine.

If you are talking about more than one "other" or national group or peoples, you would write this:

- Those are others' opinions, not mine.
- It's the Third World peoples' problems [referring to more than one national group].

When you have words that are already plural, such as children or women, you don't first make them plural and add the apostrophe. Here's how you add the possessive:

- I went to the children's concert last night.
- I attend the same women's conference each year.

But you would say:

- I enjoy going to writers' conferences.
- Drive a block past the dancers' studio.

And with what are called "attributive nouns," you would write these without an apostrophe:

- the Lakers arena, the Department of Veterans Affairs, Diners Club, Publishers Weekly, and the Dallas Cowboys stadium

TIP FOR FICTION WRITERS: **Repetition of words and phrases within close proximity occurs a lot. Our brain sometimes defaults to a word we just used when we're writing without careful examination of our word choice. When editing, check paragraphs for these repetitions, then rewrite to eliminate them. Your prose will be fresher, stronger, and more creative.**

IT'S NOT ROCKET SCIENCE!

After coming across the non-word *its'* (with an apostrophe) for the *n*th time, I decided I needed to make a statement that I'm hoping most of you already know: *It's* is not rocket science.

Why do writer complicate the *it* issue? With most all other words, deciding when to use an apostrophe + *s* or an *s* + apostrophe can be a little daunting. But really, with *it's*, it's just plain simple:

The word *it's* ONLY means "it is." It's a contraction. That's it.

You have to be able to replace *it* with "it is." Period. End of discussion.

Any other usage of *its* leaves out the apostrophe. *Its* is an adjective; *it is* is a noun and a verb. There is no word *its'*. (How would you pronounce that—"itzes"?)

Correct:

- A dog bites its fleas
- Its icing was dripping down the sides
- The boat had its motor pulled
- It's about time we writers got this down!

Like I said—it's not rocket science. Too bad not all words needing apostrophes follow this simple rule.

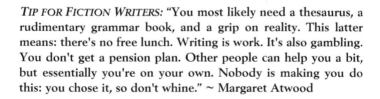

TIP FOR FICTION WRITERS: "You most likely need a thesaurus, a rudimentary grammar book, and a grip on reality. This latter means: there's no free lunch. Writing is work. It's also gambling. You don't get a pension plan. Other people can help you a bit, but essentially you're on your own. Nobody is making you do this: you chose it, so don't whine." ~ Margaret Atwood

TO ITALICIZE OR NOT TO ITALICIZE. A RULE OF THUMB

Writers need to know what types of terms are put in italics.

Think in terms of relative size. Titles of shorter works are not italicized but go in quotes. A short story title would be in quotes, but a short story anthology with many stories would have an italicized title. Titles of songs, poems, unpublished works, articles are in quotes. An epic poem's title is in italics, though, so I suppose it's up to you to decide if it's sufficiently long enough to merit the italics.

Here's a partial list of the things that need to be italicized:

- Titles of photographs
- Titles of art exhibits
- Titles of blogs (the main title used each time, not the web URL)
- Titles of podcast programs
- Title of a painting
- Title of a book
- Title of a movie
- Title of a play
- Title of a pamphlet or report
- Title of a music album or CD
- A foreign term (if you use it repeatedly, only italicize it the first time. Do not italicize a foreign name like Fifi LaPlant or a foreign city or street name.)

Note: the name of a website is just in regular headline style: "I like to browse Technium.com for new tech tips."

TIP FOR FICTION WRITERS: **Be careful when using a lot of pronouns in paragraphs that have two or more characters of the same sex. If you say "he went to his house and saw his sister," it won't be clear which "he" and "his" you are talking about. In those instances, use characters' names.**

A FRIEND OF YOURS

Are you a friend of John or a friend of John's? Often writers will leave off the "possessive" apostrophe + *s*, but you need it. Think about these two phrases:

- A portrait of King Henry
- A portrait of King Henry's

In the first instance, you have a portrait of the king. In the second instance, the king owns a portrait. There's a huge difference in meaning here. So are you a friend of John? No, you are John's friend—a friend of John's. And hopefully, he is a friend of yours (not a friend of you).

Here's another thought:

Would you say "This is one of my client's books" or "This is one of my clients' [plural] books"?

Think about it. If you have one client you are speaking about, who may have many books, the first example is correct. If you have a lot of clients (or more than one), and you are referring to one book of the many books all your clients write, then the second example is correct.

To help you decide what's correct in situations like this, try changing the word order or rewrite:

- One of my clients [plural] wrote this book. It's one of my clients' books.
- My client wrote this book; it's one of many she wrote. This is one of my client's [her] books.

One little bit of punctuation can change meaning or muddle it. So pay attention to where you place those apostrophes.

TIP FOR FICTION WRITERS: **Writers often get creative when denoting a scene break. If you have more than one scene in your chapter, you only need use a # to indicate a line space. Don't leave the space blank, for that may indicate the line space is unintentional. By using the number sign, you make it clear you are moving either into a new scene or shifting POV in the ongoing scene.**

NOTES

NOTES

STYLE AND USAGE

UTHOR E. B. WHITE ONCE said: "English usage is sometimes more than mere taste, judgment, and education—sometimes it's sheer luck, like getting across the street."

Just what is "usage" and how does it differ from grammar? *Merriam-Webster* says usage is "the way in which words and phrases are actually used (as in a particular form or sense) in a language community."

Grammar is more about accurately placing words within a sentence, whereas usage deals with the meanings of words. Usage of words changes over time, even daily. Language is fluid, and fiction writers love that! We get to play with words and their meanings.

You can use a word any way you want, and a creative writer will use her words creatively—and often poetically, such that words may take on wholly new, different meanings from how they are traditionally understood. And that's wonderful.

But we want to make sure that when we use words, our readers understand the manner in which we are using them. And if we're trying to be exact and concise, and intend to use words to mean what they're mostly understood to mean in our "language community," it behooves us to learn these accepted usages.

"My spelling is Wobbly. It's good spelling but it Wobbles, and the letters get in the wrong places."

~ *Winnie-the-Pooh, A. A. Milne*

"I love writing. I love the swirl and swing of words as they tangle with human emotions."

~ *James Michener*

CONFUSABLES

ACCEPT THE INEVITABLE EXCEPTIONS

Have you noticed how often the pairs of words that are commonly confused are antonyms (opposites)? One such pair is *accept* and *except*.

Accept is always a verb, and it means to receive or agree with or say yes to.

- Melanie accepted the award for perfect attendance.
- We don't *accept* personal checks.

Except can be a verb, a preposition, or a conjunction. However it's used, its meaning is the opposite of accept. As a verb, except means to omit, exempt, or exclude. Here are some examples:

- Melanie was excepted from the scholarship recipients. (verb)
- I go to work every day except Sunday. (preposition)
- She would have gone, except it was too far away. (conjunction)
- Everyone left except for me. (preposition)

If you're unsure which verb to use, try substituting a synonym for the word you've used: *accept* – receive or agree; *except* – omit or exclude. That should clear up the confusion.

If you've mastered these, congratulations: you're an exceptional writer.

> *TIP FOR FICTION WRITERS:* "Do the most important thing first." Have you noticed how many excellent writers start writing in the morning? That's no coincidence. They work on their goals before the rest of the day gets out of control. They aren't wondering when they're going to write, and they aren't battling to "fit it in" among their daily activities because they are doing the most important thing first. That may not work for your schedule, but if you can, try it and see how it orders your day.

ARE YOU FORTUNATE OR FORTUITOUS?

Two words that appear to share a root but do not, and are therefore often used interchangeably and incorrectly are *fortuitous* and *fortunate*. Both words convey the idea of luck or chance.

Fortunate comes from the Latin root *fortunatus*, meaning "prospered, prosperous; lucky, happy." *Fortuitous*, on the other hand, comes from the Latin root *forte*, which means "by chance." With *fortuitous*, the incident or coincident may be good or bad—fortunate or unfortunate. It's a matter of unplanned, accidental events coming together to create a desirable or undesirable outcome.

Take a look at these examples:

- It was fortuitous [a chance happening] that Mom stopped by just after the babysitter canceled for the evening. Fortunately, she had no plans for the evening and was delighted to babysit her adorable grandchild.

- A series of fortuitous events conspired against the timely sale of their home—rising interest rates, an earthquake, and their realtor's lingering illness.

Beware of using *fortuitous* with words like *accident* or *coincidence*. Accidents or coincidences are always fortuitous—chance happenings. To speak of a fortuitous accident or a fortuitous coincidence is repeating the obvious or being redundant.

You're fortunate that I'm alerting you to this now before you make an unfortunate error.

> *TIP FOR FICTION WRITERS:* Author Jodi Picoult says, "Writer's block is having too much time on your hands. If you have a limited amount of time to write, you just sit down and do it. You might not write well every day, but you can always edit a bad page. You can't edit a blank page."

MORE CONFUSION

Here are a few more sets of words that writers often get confused. First, let's take a look at a*dverse* and *averse*.

I admit to being *averse* to these two words since they often muddle me up.

To be *adverse* to something is to be in opposition to it (think: "I'm opposed to"). It's a phrase that usually refers to things, not people.

- "I'm adverse to war, poverty, and cruelty."

Averse usually describes a person's attitude, something you have feelings against. It's a subtle difference.

- "I'm averse to risk."

Two other words to examine are *effect* and *affect*. These words get confused because *effect* and *affect* can both be used as nouns or verbs. Keep in mind that usually *effect* is used as a noun and *affect* as a verb. That is a good place to start.

When *effect* is used as a verb, it means to cause something to come into being: "We can *effect* change." Otherwise the word *effect* is a noun.

- The movie had a profound effect on them.

Affect as a verb means these things:

- To act on or influence: The noise affected his hearing.
- To move emotionally: His illness affected her.
- To imitate or pretend: He affected compassion but didn't feel a thing.

Affect as a noun is described in *Merriam-Webster* as "a set of observable manifestations of a subjectively experienced emotion."

- The patient showed normal reactions and affects.

I hope these explanations did not affect you adversely.

DON'T ELICIT ILLICIT BEHAVIOR

When Brad Paisley and Carrie Underwood opened the 2013 Country Music Awards with a parody on Obamacare, one website posted: "This isn't the first time Paisley and Underwood have used a current controversy to illicit laughs and applause during a CMA opening."

The musicians' routine did just what they wanted it to do. It made people laugh. That is, it *elicited* or drew out the response they wanted. And there was nothing illicit or illegal about it. It was simply done to make people laugh over something that many people were already making fun of. Like many other "confusables," it's common to see words that sound somewhat alike misused at every turn.

Funny how such a small difference in spelling makes such a big difference in meaning.

- Use *elicit* when you mean bring about, draw out, evoke, motivate.
- Use *illicit* to describe something that is unlawful, criminal, or immoral. (If it helps, remember *illicit* starts with *ill*, so link that thought with *ill advised*.)

Speaking of immoral or illegal, do you know the difference between *vice* and *vise* ? *Vice* is a moral fault or failing, a bad habit. The *vice* squad is the department in law enforcement that is charged with enforcing laws against gambling, pornography, prostitution, and illegal drug and alcohol use. I often see writers talk about being "squeezed in a vice grip." But that makes me conjure up the image of a team of cops closing in on a criminal who's got drugs hidden in his pocket.

- A *vice* is the opposite of virtue–conforming to a certain standard of morality or a commendable quality or trait.
- A *vise* is a tool that holds or grips things.

If your only vice is not knowing how to use a vise, consider yourself virtuous.

TIP FOR FICTION WRITERS: "A good novel tells us the truth about its hero, but a bad novel tells us the truth about its author." ~ G. K. Chesterton

ARE YOU SURE IT'S ENSURE?

Don't you hate it when two words not only sound alike (homophones) but also have similar meanings? What's a writer to do? I'd like to assure you that there is a difference between *insure* and *ensure*. I find the easiest way to differentiate the two words is to think of insurance, something we all have to pay money for (often more money than we really want to pay).

Insure means to protect against loss. Example:

- I'm going to insure the shipment for $5,000.
- *Ensure* means to make sure, to make certain, to guarantee. Example:
- I will ensure that the shipment arrives by Friday.

Assure means to give the person confidence, to inform positively. The object of the verb *assure* should always refer to a person. Example: I assure you, we'll do all that's possible to get the shipment there by Friday.

I wish I could assure you that you have the necessary insurance, but in order to ensure that you do, I would have to see your policy. Make sense?

> *TIP FOR FICTION WRITERS:* Mystery author P. D. James says, "Increase your word power. Words are the raw material of our craft. The greater your vocabulary, the more effective your writing. We who write in English are fortunate to have the richest and most versatile language in the world. Respect it. Read widely and with discrimination. Bad writing is contagious."

> *TIP FOR FICTION WRITERS:* Will Self says, "Always carry a notebook. And I mean *always.* The short-term memory only retains information for three minutes; unless it is committed to paper you can lose an idea forever." A good tip for those of you who drive a lot and come up with ideas while focusing on the road (I hope) is to record ideas using your smartphone. Many have a memo recorder, so just turn it on and churn those ideas out while you drive.

NO, YOUR SPELL-CHECKER PROBABLY WON'T CATCH THESE

Here's another list of some confusables I come across regularly in my editing work. I admit, I will often look words up just to make sure I'm not confused and using the wrong spelling. Two of the biggest offenders, for me, are pallet/palette/palate and hoard/horde.

- A pallet is a shaping tool used by a potter, or it can be a platform used as a bed, or a movable structure on which bricks and bags of soil (you've seen them at the nursery) can be stacked and lifted with a forklift.
- A palette is the board artists use to mix paints.
- A palate is either the roof of your mouth or your "taste" ("this food is too spicy for my palate").
- A horde of people may want to hoard food if they are afraid of running out.

Here are a few more confusables for your consideration:

- permissible (allowable)/permissive (giving permission)
- slight (scant or many other various meanings)/sleight (only used with the expression "sleight of hand"—adeptness in a magic trick or some other deception)
- blond (adjective to describe the hair color)/blonde (only used as a noun for a female with blond hair)
  elude (avoid or evade)/allude (refer to, as in "he alluded to my story")

TIP FOR FICTION WRITERS: Not all mistakes in a novel are grammatical. Writing a book is a long process, so it is easy for writers to lose track of some of the minor plot details. However, it is vital that a writer make every effort to maintain consistency throughout the writing process because readers will notice mistakes. If you tell your readers that a character has blue eyes in the opening chapter, and then six chapters later you say they are green, the reader will remember. The solution? Use *character reference sheets*. These are simply lists of the key aspects for all of your characters—age, description, eye color, etc. Also include any details that might be important, such as specific phrases they say or mannerisms.

SOME MORE CONFUSABLES

Here are some more confusing pairs of words that you might want to pay attention to. In these kinds of words, remember that the letter C sounds the way it does in the word *ice* and the letter S like a Z—as in the word *size*:

- Advice and Advise: You give advice (noun) and you advise (verb) a friend to not drink and drive.
- Device and Devise: If you can't get that device (noun) to work, you might try to devise (verb) a plan to jerry-rig it.

Another common mix-up I've seen is with the use of *prophecy* and *prophesy*. It's easy to keep this straight if you remember the letter C sounds like *see*.

A prophet sees a prophecy (noun).

- But he will sigh when he prophesies (a good way to remember the difference).

And I often see something like "He prophesized." There is no such word, but people (including pastors at the pulpit) say it a lot.

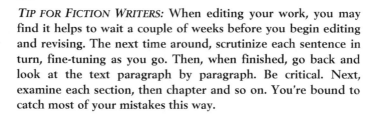

> *TIP FOR FICTION WRITERS:* When editing your work, you may find it helps to wait a couple of weeks before you begin editing and revising. The next time around, scrutinize each sentence in turn, fine-tuning as you go. Then, when finished, go back and look at the text paragraph by paragraph. Be critical. Next, examine each section, then chapter and so on. You're bound to catch most of your mistakes this way.

ARE YOU ALTOGETHER ALL TOGETHER?

A troublesome pair of confusables is *all together* and *altogether*. Note that one is a phrase and the other a single adverb.

All together is the adverb phrase meaning "in a group" or "everyone."

- The neighbors went caroling all together.
- MaryLou's soprano led the group. "All together now. Let's start with 'Joy to the World.'"

Altogether is also an adverb that means "entirely" or "completely."

- They were altogether exhausted after walking through the snow drifts and singing for an hour.

- It can also mean "all included," "all counted," or "all told."

- There were twenty-two carolers altogether.

- Or, "on the whole," or "all things considered."

- Altogether, they considered the evening a success.

If you can substitute *completely* or *all in* for *altogether*, you've got the right word. But if you can rewrite the sentence using *all together* separately, then that's the way to go.

Here is another set of words that are often confusing—*All ready* and *already*. One is an adjective phrase and one is an adverb. And the fact that I told you one is a phrase is a big hint.

All ready is an adjective phrase meaning completely ready.

- MaryLou was all ready for Christmas by December 15.

Already is an adverb that means prior to a specified or implied time, or as early as now.

- "Have you wrapped the gifts already?" Alan wailed. (so soon?)
- "The gifts were already wrapped and under the tree last week," MaryLou explained.

By now you should be altogether tired of reading this entry and already thinking about getting a snack.

THE DANGER OF MISUSE IS IMMINENT

I give extra brownie points to writers who can keep these three words straight: *imminent*, *eminent*, and *immanent*. Maybe you didn't even know there were three words like this, all with different meanings. They sound so alike, it really gives one pause—including me. So when I come across one of these, I have to run through all three in my head to make sure the correct word is being used in context.

Here are the definitions of these words:

- *Imminent*: certain and very near. "You are in imminent danger!"
- *Eminent*: distinguished, famous, or standing out, prominent. "Don't you recognize that eminent doctor?" (eminent and prominent each have only one *m*.)
- *Immanent*: indwelling, inherent (usually a theological term). "The immanent goodness of God." (You'll have to figure out a way to remember this one.)

How about this: "The eminent Reverend Smith will be giving his discourse imminently on the immanent power of the Holy Spirit."

It helps me to keep them straight by remembering that *imminent* begins the same as *immediate* (imm). And those other two words . . . well, I end up looking them up to check—for good measure.

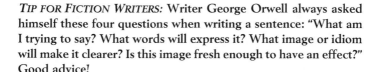

> *TIP FOR FICTION WRITERS:* Writer George Orwell always asked himself these four questions when writing a sentence: "What am I trying to say? What words will express it? What image or idiom will make it clearer? Is this image fresh enough to have an effect?" Good advice!

ARE YOU PREDOMINANTLY CORRECT OR MISTAKEN?

I sometimes hear or read sentences like "He predominately goes to that Starbuck's." That word is a mouthful, and because it sounds so much like *predominantly*, it's no surprise the words get mixed up.

While the meanings of the two words are nearly identical, there is a rationale for the differentiation.

- *Predominate*: to hold advantage in numbers or quantity; to exert controlling power or influence
- *Predominant*: having superior strength, influence or authority; being most frequent or common. (*Merriam-Webster*)

Predominate is best used as a verb, though historically it has also been used as an adjective. *Predominant*, however, is always used as an adjective. Both words are formed from the root *dominate*, for which verb and adjective usages are clearer.

I trust few of us would stumble over these word choices:

- Ranchers' interests dominate the Western Governors Conference agenda.
- The dominant concern of the Western Governors Conference is ranching interests.

History is against the critics. *Predominate* has been recorded as an adjective since 1591. It's true that *predominantly* is much more common than *predominately*, as *predominant* is than *predominate*. However, there is no difference in sense between the pairs, and the other forms aren't wrong, just less often preferred alternatives.

When the adverb is called for, *predominantly* wins out almost every time, even though both *predominate* and *predominant* can be turned into adverbs by adding *ly*. But *predominantly* predominates in good usage.

TIP FOR FICTION WRITERS: F. Scott Fitzgerald gave this great advice: "Cut out all these exclamation points. An exclamation point is like laughing at your own joke." Excessive punctuation, like using all caps, can come across as yelling at the reader. Let the context imply the emotion.

ARE YOU LIKELY OR APT TO READ THIS?

Here are four words that are often confused: *apt, likely, prone, liable*. Their differences are a bit subtle, but they do mean different things, so you might want to pay attention to these for future reference.

- *Apt*: Means one is habitually inclined. A frog is apt to gobble up a fly if it gets too close.
- *Likely*: Means one is inclined or tending toward something. She is likely to win [implying the odds are with her].
- *Prone*: Means one is inclined, but usually implies undesirable results. He's prone to tripping.
- *Liable*: Means one is likely to suffer, and always undesirable consequences. She's liable to have accidents [implies probability].

These words have no bearing on other meanings of these words, such as *a likely story, he's lying prone, she's an apt pupil, not liable for the accident* (legally responsible).

Being a copyeditor, I'm apt to look for misuse of these words! And I'm likely to find some!

> *TIP FOR FICTION WRITERS:* Author Tracy Kidder gives good advice to novelists: "Try to attune yourself to the sound of your own writing. If you can't imagine yourself saying something aloud, then you probably shouldn't write it."

ARE YOU EAGER OR ANXIOUS?

Despite the fact that they are often used interchangeably (and *Merriam-Webster* calls them synonyms), *anxious* and *eager* do not mean the same thing. "Both words convey the notion of being desirous," says Theodore Bernstein in *The Careful Writer*, "but *anxious* has an underlay of faint apprehension."

Anxious means worry, concern, distress, uneasiness—all negative connotations.

- Marie was anxious as she waited for the doctor's diagnosis.

Those who argue that *anxious* should never be used as a synonym for *eager* overstate their case. *Webster's New College Dictionary* includes this definition for *anxious*: eagerly wishing.

If that's the sense you wish to convey, it's an appropriate use of the word.

- Henrietta was anxious to see her new grandchild.

In the case of a much-anticipated child, the concern over the child's safe delivery and eagerness to see the new baby make *anxious* the right word to use. And that is always our goal as writers—to use the precise word.

Eager conveys enthusiasm, inpatient desire, or interest. *Eager* has an air of expecting something good.

- Marie was eager for a good report.
- The children were eager for summer vacation.

Sometimes I am too eager to express my opinion, and that makes me anxious about the response from my peers.

TIP FOR FICTION WRITERS: "Easy reading is damn hard writing. But if it's right, it's easy. It's the other way round, too. If it's slovenly written, then it's hard to read. It doesn't give the reader what the careful writer can give the reader." ~ Maya Angelou

ALTERNATING BETWEEN ALTERNATIVES

There seems to be some confusion over the words *alternate* and *alternative*. Can they be used interchangeably? Does *alternative* involve only two choices? The confusion is understandable, since both words serve multiple parts of speech.

Alternate can be a verb, noun, or adjective. When used as a verb, the last syllable is accented and the final *a* is long.

- Verb: Joan and I alternated sitting in the front seat to keep our motion sickness under control. (Meaning: took turns)
- Noun: The alternates to the political convention were vocal in their opposition to the taxation bill. (Meaning: substitutes)
- Adjective: We took an alternate route to the museum due to construction.(Meaning: another option/choice)

Alternative can be a noun or an adjective.

- Noun: My morning alternative to coffee is a headache. (Meaning: a choice—caffeine or headache)
- Adjective: *Lolapalooza* began as a showcase for alternative bands in the early 1990s. (Meaning: another choice, option)

Some argue that *alternative* refers only to two choices. Such reasoning is a logical progression from the word's Latin root *alter*, meaning "the other of two." But there is nearly universal agreement that *alternative* can refer to multiple options.

Both *Merriam-Webster* and the *American Heritage Dictionary* define *alternative* as involving two or more choices. So writing "the alternatives available to a Starbuck's customer are limitless" is correct, if not overwhelming.

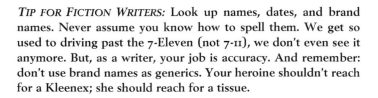

TIP FOR FICTION WRITERS: **Look up names, dates, and brand names. Never assume you know how to spell them. We get so used to driving past the 7-Eleven (not 7-11), we don't even see it anymore. But, as a writer, your job is accuracy. And remember: don't use brand names as generics. Your heroine shouldn't reach for a Kleenex; she should reach for a tissue.**

ARE YOU DONE OR FINISHED?

A child pushes a plate away at the end of the meal and announces, "I'm done."

The well-intentioned but misinformed parent chides, "You're *finished*, dear. Cakes are *done*. People are finished."

Are they? Is there a rule that tells when to use *done* and when to use *finished*?

According to the *Oxford English Dictionary*, *done* has been accepted and used in good company as the past tense of *do* dating back to the 1300s. There seems to have been some preference or practice for using *have* with *done* and *be/am* verbs only with *finished*.

It's also worth noting that *finished* is a more recent term, dating only to the 1700s. So the insistence on using *done* only in reference to things and *finished* only to people is really a stubborn refusal to acknowledge the reality that languages are living, breathing, and changing things.

Modern dictionaries agree. Most define *done* first as a past form of *do*, which means to accomplish or complete an effort. *Done*, meaning "cooked adequately," is much further down the list. But this does show that, yes, people can be both done and/or finished.

However, *finished* implies an object (called a transitive verb) in this type of structure. Finished what? Dinner. Finished with what? With eating.

But when using *finished* as an intransitive verb (not needing an object), it can also mean something like "I'm washed up," "done for [there's *done* again]," "I'm toast [okay, slang, but you get the idea]." Which gets me thinking about *done* and how it describes the degree something (like a cut of meat) is cooked. Can you be "well done" with your dinner?

So go right ahead and excuse yourself from the table with an "I'm done." And don't let anyone tell you you're finished instead of done. Unless they really mean you are washed up.

ARE YOU IRRITATED OR AGGRAVATED?

Does it *irritate* you when people use *aggravate* when they mean annoy? Or are you just confused about the correct use of these two words?

Aggravate comes from Latin, and if you look carefully you'll see its root—*grave*. The original meaning was to make heavy or increase the burden. Over the years the meaning and usage morphed into meaning "to make worse or more serious," or "to intensify."

- The spicy chili aggravated Malcolm's colitis.

But *aggravate* can also mean annoy or exasperate—synonyms for *irritate*. In fact, that meaning came into use about the same time as the previous meaning.

Some purists maintain that using *aggravate* to mean anything other than *to worsen* blurs its distinctive meaning. Others argue that the use of *aggravate* to indicate *a worsening of one's temper* is a legitimate use of the word.

- Eleanor was irritated by the incessant elevator music.
- The incessant elevator music was an aggravation (annoyance) to Eleanor.

Either sentence is correct. As a writer, be sure the word you use conveys your intended meaning. Understand that *aggravate* means worsen, and be careful about using it as a synonym for *irritate*.

I hope I didn't irritate you with this explanation. I would hate to aggravate your stress!

> *TIP FOR FICTION WRITERS:* Barbara Kingsolver says, "I write a lot of material that I know I'll throw away. It's just part of the process. I have to write hundreds of pages before I get to page one." Be willing to write badly at times, but be determined to set times to dig in and rewrite or toss the pages. Every writer is different, but if you cling to every word you write, you won't improve in your writing."

I BOTH ANTICIPATE AND EXPECT A REACTION

Here's a pair of words that share similar nuances: anticipate and expect. Both mean to look forward to. But anticipate also carries the idea of taking action in expectation or preparation for a future event. Expect carries more certainty and does not require action.

- The Johnsons anticipated a long winter. (They took steps to prepare, perhaps stocking a cellar with canned goods, having supplies of heating fuel, etc.)
- The Morgans expected a long winter. (They were certain of what lay ahead, but the sentence implies no preparations.)

Expect also has other meanings. *Expecting* is often used to refer to pregnancy. A couple who is planning to start a family may anticipate being pregnant by a certain time, but once the pregnancy is certain, we talk about expecting a baby. Barring any complications, the arrival of a baby is an almost certain probability.

Expect can also mean something that is required.

- I expect your chores to be done when I come home.
- His parents expected him to excel in school.

Now that you know the difference, I expect you will use these terms correctly in the future. Although, I'll anticipate your future need for more Say What? posts in my blog.

TIP FOR FICTION WRITERS: In American English, we usually leave off the "st" and say *amid,* not *amidst.* And we say *among,* not amongst. So if you live in the US, you may be "*among* a great number of Americans who use *amid* instead of *amidst.*"

A FEW MISUSED WORDS I CAN ACCOST YOU WITH

I like to keep a list of words that are used incorrectly; some of these may surprise you:

- *Accost.* The word has no reference to physical contact. It means to approach and speak to someone in an abrupt or challenging manner.
- *Decimate.* Writers often misuse this word, which has its root in *deci*, or ten. The original meaning was "to kill one in ten." This meaning faded over time, but its true use now is to cause a great loss of life or to destroy a large part of something. It never means to complete annihilate (use that word instead, if that's your intent).
- *Enormity.* This word is almost always confused with enormousness, and the problem is that enormity predominantly means a monstrous, vicious, immoral act—a very negative connotation. So if you say something like "I was overwhelmed with the enormity of arranging my daughter's wedding," you would be tainting the event in a way that you might not want. Lots of people make this mistake.

You might feel that if everyone is using a word incorrectly, and the accepted meaning of a word has changed and is now accepted in society to mean something different, then it's fine to use it incorrectly. Well, being a copyeditor and a handler of words, my feeling is no, we shouldn't.

Garner's wonderful reference book *Garner's Modern American Usage* (which I use a lot) rates words and phrases (on a scale of one to five) as to how accepted they have become with their "new" usage. Some words have fully changed so that they mean something much different from their original meaning. This happens all the time and is part and parcel of the way language evolves, and that's to be expected.

But until a word reaches "stage five," which means it's wholly acceptable, it's best to use the word in its original or traditional sense. Using a dictionary like *Merriam-Webster's Collegiate 11th Edition* will also help you discern whether you are using a word correctly. I love having that dictionary loaded on my computer with the icon on my task bar. I keep the program open all day as I work, and refer to it often. You might try it and like it.

NEGLECT, IGNORE, OR DISREGARD THIS AT YOUR PERIL!

English grammar and spelling are confusing, but they pale in comparison to explaining the subtle differences and appropriate usage of some synonyms. For example, *thrifty, frugal,* and *miserly* could all be used to describe someone who is careful with their resources. I consider myself thrifty, even frugal when necessary; others may consider me miserly. It's often a matter of perspective and relativity when choosing which of several words to use when they carry a similar meaning.

Neglect, ignore, and *disregard* present a similar conundrum. They all include the concept of not paying attention to someone or something. *Merriam-Webster* includes "to leave undone or unattended to, especially through carelessness."

- *Neglect* is failure to tend to someone or something for which you are responsible. Neglect takes place over a period of time and carries predictable consequences. Neglected neighborhoods fall prey to economic blight; neglected children fail to thrive physically as well as emotionally.

- In contrast, *ignore* is generally a one-time incident. If an old flame shows up at a party, you may "refuse to take notice" of him or her. If someone insults you or your work, you may choose to overlook or ignore the remark by not responding or pretending not to have heard it. Neglect would be inappropriate in these instances because these are in-the-moment occurrences.

- *Disregard* applies to things, often abstractions, but not people. The word carries the additional meaning of unworthiness. You may disregard something that you don't feel is worthy of notice—someone's advice, or overly restrictive neighborhood standards. If you live in a controlled neighborhood, you may find some of the restrictions burdensome, but disregard them at your peril.

Neglect and *disregard* always carry negative connotations; *ignore* is not necessarily negative.

I may ignore my children on occasion, but I should never neglect them. And I try not to disregard the things they say to me. They may have something important to teach me. I hope I've taught you something valuable as well, that you won't want to either ignore or disregard!

NOTES

NOTES

NOTES

WORD MEANINGS AND USAGE

ARE YOU LITERALLY BEING LITERAL?

How many times have you heard people throw the word *literally* around? It's one of those words that has become common to use, but few really think about what the word actually means. And probably quite a few don't really care.

But we writers should care about the literal meaning of the word *literally*, and try to understand the difference between *literal* and *literally*. We hear or read expressions like these:

- "My eyes literally popped out of my head."
- "That was literally the worst party ever!"
- "I literally had to use a knife to cut through that whipped cream."

The word *literally* means "in a literal sense or manner." *Literal* means "completely true and accurate" or "free from exaggeration." At least that's one definition listed by Merriam-Webster's dictionary. Another definition is this: "in effect; virtually." And there's a nice little note indicating that some people frequently criticize definition number two as a misuse of the word because it seems the opposite of sense number one—with good reason, I say, because it is.

Is something literal when it is perfectly accurate or when it's only seemingly accurate? Seems like it can't be both. Which makes me think of how we might say something is way cool or totally hot—and don't get me started on expressions like "drawing the blinds" or words like *bimonthly* (which can mean either twice a month or every two months . . .).

If you ask me, this is yet another word that has been so long misused in common practice that it's become accepted, much like the now-accepted word *ain't* instead of *aren't* or *isn't*. It's true that English is a constantly evolving language, but this word, in my opinion, is one that is literally better left alone.

> *Tip for Fiction Writers:* Author A. J. Jacobs says, "Force yourself to generate dozens of ideas. A lot of those ideas will be terrible. Most of them, in fact. But there will be some sparkling gems in there too. Try to set aside twenty minutes a day just for brainstorming."

AMID AND AMONG

Writers often get mass nouns and count nouns confused. The preposition among is used with count nouns—meaning you use it with things you can actually count:

- "I stood among a group of friends."

The preposition *amid* is used with mass nouns, meaning you use it with things you can't count. You would say:

- "I wandered through the city amid the noise and smog, until I found myself among strangers, who looked at me oddly."

Amid often has the sense of being in the middle of something, or being surrounded, whereas *among* is more an intermingling or mixing with distinct or separate objects.

> *TIP FOR FICTION WRITERS:* Author George Orwell advised following these rules: "Never use a long word where a short one will do. If it is possible to cut a word out, always cut it out. Never use the passive where you can use the active. Never use a foreign phrase, a scientific word, or a jargon word if you can think of an everyday English equivalent."

HOPEFULLY, YOU'LL LEARN SOMETHING FROM THIS ENTRY

Or, to be more correct, the title should read "I hope you will learn something from this entry."

Back in the 1600s, this word *hopefully* was first used in the English language to denote "something that is done in a hopeful manner." As in "She hopefully gazed out the tower window for her prince to come rescue her."

About a hundred years later, someone decided it would be a good idea to use the word in a different way: "Hopefully, the war will be over soon." The word *hopefully*, in this case, is little more than a substitute for "I hope."

This sense of the word didn't really catch on in common usage until somewhere around the middle of the twentieth century, but by the 1960s, it was firmly entrenched in the English lexicon. While not technically grammatically incorrect (it fits into a class of adverbs called disjuncts), it does sometimes present a bit of a problem. Consider this example:

- Hopefully, my sister's ankle will heal in time for her to go to the skating party.

For most of us, it's not that difficult to parse the sentence and identify the origin of the well-wishing—the speaker him/herself, right? But consider the fact that the speaker's sister most certainly is wishing the same thing. So, does the "hopefully" apply to the speaker, or to the sister, or to both? See how much clearer it would be to just say "I hope," if indeed the healing was hoped for by the speaker?

Worded another way, the sentence (and the usage of *hopefully*) becomes even more ambiguous:

- My sister's ankle will hopefully heal in time for her to go to the skating party.

This sentence is grammatically just as correct as the previous one, and it contains all the same words, but it becomes even more difficult to parse. It is worded in such a way that it almost seems, at first glance, that the "hopefully" could be referring to the ankle itself. Ankles, of course, do not have the cognitive power to hope. Therefore, that interpretation just isn't possible, although it is implied by the wording.

Again, it would have been so much less problematic to just say "I hope," since that's what was probably meant by saying "hopefully" in that sentence anyway. Doing so only adds one more word, but it cuts out an "*ly*" word, and it aids in clearing up sentence ambiguity. And the main goal of all your writing should be clarity, above all else. I hope that this discussion clears up any confusion over the use of the word *hopefully*!

PROVED VS. PROVEN

Here are two words that seem to be interchangeable. But there is a bit of a difference in usage with *proved* and *proven*. And there's a simple rule to knowing which to use when.

Use *proven* only as an adjective (remember, an adjective describes a noun). Use *proved* as a verb.

Correct examples:

- Her prediction proved true.
- She proved she was smarter than he.
- That strategy is a proven failure.
- He was the proven champion.

Merriam-Webster says this: "As a past participle, *proven* is now about as frequent as *proved* in all contexts. As an attributive adjective (proved or proven gas reserves), *proven* is much more common than *proved*."

Okay, you're asking what an "attributive adjective" is. It's an adjective that comes directly before the noun it describes. Simple. Remember: adjectives describe a noun. The word *guaranteed* is an attributive adjective in the phrase "guaranteed sales." Adverbs modify a verb.

TIP FOR FICTION WRITERS: Here's a challenging tip for writers. Are you up to it? "I write while walking on a treadmill. I started this practice when I was working on *Drop Dead Healthy,* and read all these studies about the dangers of the sedentary life. Sitting is alarmingly bad for you. One doctor told me that 'sitting is the new smoking.' So I bought a treadmill and put my computer on top of it. It took me about 1,200 miles to write my book. I kind of love it—it keeps me awake, for one thing." ~ A. J. Jacobs

APPARENTLY

Let's take a look at one word: *Apparent.* This word means "seeming." I've said this before: even though we may say certain phrases in conversation and it's accepted, that doesn't make it okay to use it in your writing (unless you want a character to say this incorrectly, on purpose). Dialog and even internalizing allows for characters to say and think things that are grammatically incorrect.

In one of my novels I have a jerky character who always says "sayings" wrong. I had him yell to another person, "Why don't you crawl back under that rock you came out of?" My line editor corrected me and said it made no sense, and she missed the point that I had made him look like an idiot on purpose.

But that's characterization, and this is the "real" world of correct usage of the English language, so . . .

You can't die of an "apparent" heart attack (although it seems many characters in novels do). You can *apparently* die of a heart attack.

Wrong:

- She is dead of an apparent suicide.

Correct:

- She apparently died of suicide.

Apparently, most people don't know this is the correct usage for the word *apparent.*

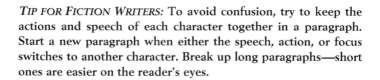

> *TIP FOR FICTION WRITERS:* **To avoid confusion, try to keep the actions and speech of each character together in a paragraph. Start a new paragraph when either the speech, action, or focus switches to another character. Break up long paragraphs—short ones are easier on the reader's eyes.**

PASS THE COLLOCATIONS

Collocations. Isn't that a neat word? It refers to regular pairings of words, and boy, there are many I use incorrectly and have to look up. Problem is, we get so lazy and weird in our speech that we've accepted many pairings that are just plain wrong. So I'm going to give you a list of the correct pairings for certain phrases we regularly use. There are myriad, but I'm going to pick the ones I like.

- Abide with: I abide with my husband.
- Absolve by: I was absolved by the judge.
- Absolve from: And he absolved me from the penalties.
- Accord with: I'm in accord with the new policies at work.
- Account to: You will have to account to the principal for what you did.
- Account for: He must account for his actions.
- Advise of: She advised me of the rules.
- Advise about: You need to advise me about the issue soon. (And be careful not to mix up *advise* and *advice*, which many do!)
- Agreeable to: He's agreeable to my plan.
- Agreeable with: Your idea is agreeable with mine.
- Answer to: You must answer to your parents.
- Answer for: I have to answer for my crimes.
- Averse to: He is averse to seeing scary movies.

As you probably noticed, I only covered the letter A—which should give you a clue about how many there are.

TIP FOR FICTION WRITERS: Vary the length and style of sentences so your writing doesn't sound boring or stilted. Look at the first word of every sentence in a paragraph. If you spot more than two that begin with the same pronoun, such as *he, she, it, I,* etc., consider rewording some. Find ways to change a statement into a question or use a partial sentence for variation. Try to avoid using the same adjective or verb in a paragraph as well. A reader will catch that repetition, and repetition smacks of lazy or uncreative writing.

MORE COOL COLLOCATIONS

No, a collocation is not a vegetable you steam and eat with butter. A collocation is a word pairing, and there are certain verbs that should be paired with specific prepositions. So here are some more collocations—which might be fun to eat while munching on a green leafy vegetable:

- Center upon: Center your attention upon his theme. [*center around* is incorrect]
- Cause for: This is no cause for alarm.
- Compatible with: She is not very compatible with her boyfriend, in my opinion.
- Consideration for: You should have consideration for others.
- Consideration of: In consideration of the circumstances, maybe you should leave.
- Depends on: That depends on whether or not he is telling the truth.
- Depends upon: His life depends upon his telling the truth.
- Differ from: You differ from me in looks.
- Differ with: I beg to differ with you.
- Enamored of: He is enamored of his fiancée (bet you didn't know this one).
- Incorrect in: She was incorrect in her answer.
- Oblivious to: You are oblivious to my needs.
- You can preside at or over a meeting.

You can now jump at the chance to stop reading this, but don't jump to conclusions thinking this is the last you'll hear about collocations. However, rest easy—I am done for now.

> *TIP FOR FICTION WRITERS:* Keep an eye out in your writing for verbs that state existence, like *seem, feel, become,* and *look* (appeared). While they certainly have a place in writing, often using these verbs tell instead of show. Instead of saying "he feels angry," think of ways to show that anger in physical ways. You can do a search for these verbs to take a look at the context. If you can replace one of these "existence" verbs for a stronger one that shows instead of tells, all the better.

ARE YOU INFERRING OR IMPLYING?

I found a very nice explanation online that tells the difference between the words *infer* and *imply*. "You imply things through your own words. You infer things from someone else's words." The speaker implies. The listener infers (gets it).

When you imply something, you are initiating the action. You might be saying something that is implying something hidden in the subtext. By pointing at that chocolate bar on the rack, I'm implying to my husband that I'd like him to put one (or more) in the shopping basket. When you imply, you express something indirectly.

However, when you infer something, you are surmising, extrapolating, or deducing something from what you see or hear (or taste, smell, or touch). You experience something through your senses and you infer what it might be or mean.

You might infer that I'm lying when I say I hate chocolate. Especially if you see all the chocolate in my cupboards and on the counters.

When you tell me that, I might imply you're being a bit rude. You might then infer that I'm somewhat defensive, if not dissembling. And then I might imply it would be a good idea for you to leave my house. And so on . . .

TIP FOR FICTION WRITERS: Be consistent when using a character's name. In narrative use only one form of a character's name. For example, don't use Robert in some places and Bob in the other. The only exception is in dialog, as sometimes another character may use a nickname for that person in direct address or internal thoughts (revealed when in that character's POV).

I MAY BE WRONG, MAYBE . . .

It seems a lot of writers use *maybe* in the place of "may be" a bit too often, maybe. The word *maybe* is an adverb (do you remember what those are? They modify a verb). It means perhaps. So anytime you can use *perhaps* in the spot you want to write *maybe*, you are A-OK.

So when are you *not* supposed to use *maybe* and should use *may be* instead? Remember, *may* is a verb.

- You may go outside if I say so.
- You may do it anyway.
- You may be a bit belligerent.
- You may be tuning me out. But I'm used to it.

Think "might be" or "could be." Or maybe not.

> *TIP FOR FICTION WRITERS:* When a character is speaking for a long stretch of time in a scene with more than two characters, don't wait until the end of the long paragraph to put a speaker or narrative tag. If the reader isn't sure who is speaking, they will usually skim to the end of the paragraph before reading all the speech to figure out who is speaking, and that's a bad thing. Add either a speaker tag or narrative tag to the first sentence to make it clear right away who is speaking.

BOTH AND *ONLY* ARE FOUR-LETTER WORDS

Not *those kind of* four-letter words. But just as you might ask yourself whether *those* four-letter words are necessary, you will want to check your use of these words: *both* and *only*.

Wait, you're thinking, Isn't *both* the kind of word you need to make your writing clear? It can be. But there are also times it can create just enough confusion to make a reader stumble. And that's something you want to avoid.

Consider this sentence:

- The administration notified both teachers and parents of the pending budget dilemma.

Does *both* clarify or raise questions? In this instance, a plural noun immediately follows *both*— leaving the reader open to the possibility, even momentarily, that *both* modifies only *teachers*. It may even give the impression that the school has only two teachers.

Here *both* raises questions that distract the reader from the writer's purpose. Is anything lost when *both* is removed? No, removing it actually tightens the sentence and offers just the clarity, precision, and economy of words that all writers (should) strive for.

Here's a simple rule about this: if *both* doesn't add anything to the sentence and comes before a pair of plural nouns, you can safely remove it.

The challenge with *only* is placement. *Only* modifies the word or phrase immediately following it. A sentence's meaning will change significantly depending on where you place that little word, as this sentence illustrates:

- Only Madeleine eats chocolate when she's under stress. (Madeleine, no one else, eats chocolate under stress.)
- Madeleine eats only chocolate when she's under stress. (Madeleine doesn't eat beef jerky or chips, just chocolate when she's stressed out.)
- Madeleine eats chocolate only when she's under stress. (*Only* modifies the phrase "when she's under stress." Madeleine doesn't eat chocolate when things are going well.)
- Madeleine eats chocolate when she's under stress only. (Moving *only* to the end of the sentence does not change its meaning in the previous sentence.)

It's a good practice to always be as clear as possible in your speaking and writing, and remembering to place *only* immediately before the word it clarifies is one simple way to do that.

ARE YOU INFAMOUS OR MORE THAN FAMOUS?

I couldn't resist devoting one entry on this since one of my favorite bits in the movie *The Three Amigos* (although there are so many good bits!) is when the three actors get the urgent telegram requesting them to come down to Mexico to face the infamous El Guapo.

What follows is a little explanation from one amigo to the other, saying that *"infamous* means 'more than famous.'" For the record, in case you don't know the meaning of the word, *infamous* means having an evil reputation, or when describing an act—an infamous crime—you would be emphasizing the disgrace this act brings upon the one perpetrating it. (Should I be so bold as to say FDR was using the term incorrectly when he referred to the day of the Pearl Harbor bombing as "a day that will go down in infamy"? If you think so, check the dictionary definition of *infamy*.)

There is a slight difference, also, between *infamous* and *notorious*. Both mean "well-known for some disreputable or wicked quality, deed, or event," but

- *Notorious* emphasizes the "well-known" aspect and is often misused to just apply to famous (not infamous) individuals or events.
- *Infamous* emphasizes the wickedness aspect, and the person doesn't have to be well-known. You can have infamous behavior and be a nobody.

And if you want to delve into another "amigo" word-explanation, the bit on the meaning of *plethora* between El Guapo and his sidekick is too funny. Trust me and just watch the movie.

TIP FOR FICTION WRITERS: Check through your dialog to make sure you aren't using too many beats that break up the flow. Excessive or continual speaker and narrative tags, like "he said" or "he blinked and rubbed his neck" can become irritating. Only use a speaker tag when it's unclear who is speaking or if back-and-forth dialog between two people goes on so long the reader may lose track of who is saying what. Try to make the narrative tags meaningful so they are not just bits of random physical movements that come across only as a way to identify the speaker.

I CONTINUE TO BE CONTINUOUS

I continue to be concerned about good writing. That's why I want to point out to you that *continual* and *continuous* are not the same thing. Sure, they have the same root word: *continue*. They both refer to duration or length. But the root *continue* has many variations with slight but significant differences in meaning and usage than *continuous*.

Continuous means without stopping.

- Hannah kept up a continuous wail while Dad changed her diaper. (Poor Dad. There was no break, no reprieve, from the baby's ear-splitting cries.)

But *continual* means repeated with intermittent breaks.

- Baby Hannah's irritable disposition may have been due to continual outbreaks of diaper rash. (Her diaper rash would clear up, then return some time later—repeatedly.)

Need a visual to help you keep these two words straight? *Continual* is a dotted line—something that comes and goes, starts and stop. *Continuous* is a circle, never ending.

And your bonus word—*continuum*—is a solid line, a continuous series or a whole in which one part is indistinguishable from the next. A continuum is a collection, sequence, or progression of elements varying by minute degrees.

- The performance elicited a continuum of every emotion—from sadness to joy—and left the viewers speechless.

I will continue with continuous grammar tips to provide you with a continuum of ideas, from easy to difficult. But if you continually complain, I may have to stop.

TIP FOR FICTION WRITERS: Using unusual words that hardly anyone ever uses does not impress readers. It never calls attention to itself. Don't make your readers work hard to figure out what you're trying to say. That doesn't mean to "dumb down" your writing. But even when writing for the most literate and sophisticated of audiences, it's best to resist the urge to impress by flaunting an arcane assortment of vocabulary words.

STAY AWHILE AND I'LL EXPLAIN

I'm going to speak to you a (short) while about when to use *a while* and *awhile*. It may seem like no big deal, and really, is there a distinction?

I see writers all the time using *awhile* incorrectly. Yes, grammar and usage is about the little things, like dotting your i's and crossing your t's. Sorry. If this seems too minuscule to bother with, read another entry. But I would encourage you to take advantage of these little "lessons" to become a better writer. So stay awhile and learn something.

The word *awhile* is an adverb. That means it modifies a verb. It means "for a while" (*while* in this phrase is a noun) or "for a time," so you'd be redundant if you said, "I'd like you to stay for awhile" (which means "stay for for a time"). The key to watch for is the word *for*. You either stay for a while (a period of time) or you stay awhile (for a time).

Correct examples:

- Please stay awhile so we can talk.
- He left a while ago.

The word *while* alone can mean other things, like trouble: "It's worth your while." In fact, *while* can be used as a noun, verb, adverb, preposition, or conjunction. And this is the correct spelling of the word in the expression "to while away the hours."

Was this lesson worth your while? See, that wasn't so painful, was it?

TIP FOR FICTION WRITERS: **Author Neil Gaiman says, "Write. Put one word after another. Find the right word, put it down. Finish what you're writing. Whatever you have to do to finish it, finish it." Simple advice but not so simple to do, right? Set reasonable goals for your writing, then strive to reach them. It helps if you look at your writing as a real job—and think of yourself as a professional. Thinking and imagining is what gets you to your goal. Don't think, "I have a book inside me." Instead think, "I have a *writer* inside me."**

THE REASON WHY IS BECAUSE

Writers, pay close attention to this one. Few people ever stop to think what they are saying (or writing) when they throw all these words together in a sentence. Almost every time a writer starts with "the reason," I am sure to see the word *why* following it. Don't do that!

This is something I really didn't learn until years into my writing, but now I'm keenly aware of it. Because of the way we often talk, we make this mistake in our writing regarding *reason* and *why*.

The word *reason* means an explanation. The word *why* is defined in *Merriam-Webster's* as "cause, *reason*, or purpose." Maybe you already see where I'm going with this.

If you say, "The reason why I ate that . . . ," you are saying, "The reason reason I ate that."

Now, the word *because* means . . . you guessed it: *why*.

So now, if you say, "The reason why I ate that is because . . . ," you are saying, "The reason reason I ate that is the reason . . ." (or something close to that). Doesn't that make you want to say "arrgggh!"? That's what I say when I come upon sentences constructed like that.

Most Word options can be set to detect the *reason-why* combination and will flag it, but try to watch out for it.

That sentence, by the way, should just be "The reason I ate that sandwich is I was hungry." Or you could use two sentences: "Why did I eat that sandwich? Because I was hungry."

TIP FOR FICTION WRITERS: Author Kurt Vonnegut says, "Be a sadist. No matter how sweet and innocent your leading characters, make awful things happen to them—in order that the reader may see what they are made of." Always ask yourself how you can make things as bad as you can for your characters. That's what makes readers turn pages.

THIS ENTRY COMPRISES THREE SHORT PARAGRAPHS

Okay, this is going to be a short but concise entry here. Repeat after me:

- "The whole comprises the parts . . . the whole comprises the parts."

Writers always mess up with *comprise*. The word does *not* mean compose. You cannot say "it is comprised of." Sorry, can't.

- A house comprises six rooms.
- Six chapters are comprised in the novel.
- My novel comprises eighteen chapters.
- This blog comprises fifty-two entries for the year.

Okay, some say the word has evolved and now it's acceptable to use *comprise* to mean "compose," but as *Merriam-Webster* says: "You may be subject to criticism if you do so." Heaven forbid someone criticizes your misuse of *comprise*!

Now, my bicycle is *composed* of various metals like aluminum and steel. Or I could say my cheesecake is *made up of* ten different ingredients. This all may sound odd to your ear, but this is the correct way to use *comprise*. Comprende?

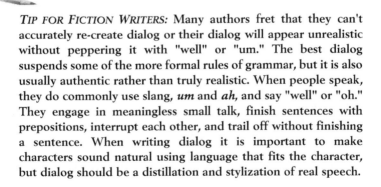

TIP FOR FICTION WRITERS: Many authors fret that they can't accurately re-create dialog or their dialog will appear unrealistic without peppering it with "well" or "um." The best dialog suspends some of the more formal rules of grammar, but it is also usually authentic rather than truly realistic. When people speak, they do commonly use slang, *um* and *ah*, and say "well" or "oh." They engage in meaningless small talk, finish sentences with prepositions, interrupt each other, and trail off without finishing a sentence. When writing dialog it is important to make characters sound natural using language that fits the character, but dialog should be a distillation and stylization of real speech.

GIVING IT REGARD

You've probably heard the phrase: "Give my regards to Broadway." That's a good line to remember when you want to know when to use the expressions "regard to" and "regards to."

The phrase *regard to* means regarding or pertaining. But, when you *give regards*, you are saying hello.

Wrong:

- This is in regards to the note I sent.
- I'm answering in regards to your concern.

Correct:

- This is in regard to the note I sent.
- I'm answering in regard to your concern.

> *TIP FOR FICTION WRITERS:* Don't use boldface or underline in your writing. Same goes for all caps. Using these font treatments is a lazy (and unacceptable) substitution for choosing strong verbs and adjectives that will convey the emotion or emphasis you want. Italics can be used to emphasize a word or phrase, but use them sparingly. Long passages of italics are hard to read and will defeat your purpose in trying to make one point stand out.

AS SMART AS A WHIP

Here is a construction that many overlook: "as-as." We tend to mess this one up a lot because we often say a sentence with this structure incorrectly. When using *as-as* construction, you have to use *as* twice—before and after the adjective.

Wrong:

- They were thick as thieves.
- She's smart as a whip.

Correct:

- They were as thick as thieves.
- She's as smart as a whip.

One exception is: "He did as best he could." *As best* is a traditional idiom (according to Bryan Gardner) that substitutes "as good as."

I hope, though, you don't use these clichés in your writing! And just how smart is a whip anyway?

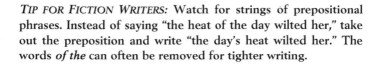

> *TIP FOR FICTION WRITERS:* Watch for strings of prepositional phrases. Instead of saying "the heat of the day wilted her," take out the preposition and write "the day's heat wilted her." The words *of the* can often be removed for tighter writing.

> *TIP FOR FICTION WRITERS:* Lack of clarity is often caused by putting too many things in one sentence. Break the sentence up and use full stops. It can also be caused by jargon and stock phrases that are meaningless. Just use plain English.

WHEN "WHERE" SHOULD BE "IN WHICH"

Writers are so used to using the word where in a general sense that I imagine many don't stop to think just what they are really saying. I'm speaking specifically in sentences like these:

- The Bible contains many verses where people can find hope.
- I heard a lecture where the instructor quoted Shakespeare excessively.
- I saw a movie where the bad guy fell out of a plane.

The word *where* pertains to a physical location, and none of the subjects in the above sentences are locations. While a lecture is given at a certain location, the sentence is speaking about the content of the lecture. In sentences like these, it is best to use *in which*. See how much more accurately these read:

- The Bible contains many verses in which people can find hope.
- I heard a lecture in which the instructor quoted Shakespeare excessively.
- I saw a movie in which the bad guy fell out of a plane.

It might be easier to remember to use *where* only when referring to a place. For example: "I went to the market, where I ran into Jim." And in all other cases you might want to use the "more formal" (but more correct) *which*: "I read a book in which is contained all the mysteries of the ancient world."

I'm all for keeping things simple, so you might reword this last sentence this way: "I read a book that contained all the mysteries . . ." But if you really can't simplify the sentence without losing the gist of what you are trying to say, be sure to check first to see if you are speaking about a location or not.

TIP FOR FICTION WRITERS: **When you use extra words in sentences, make sure they are purposeful and add deliberate meaning. Don't be lazy and just write whatever comes into your mind. Think about your genre, tone, and the voice of your character (if you are in a character's POV) with the aim to choose the best words and phrasing possible.**

EVERYDAY CONFUSION . . . EVERY DAY

Let's take a look at some words that can either be one word or broken in two. Since the meanings are usually quite different, it's important to take a closer look at these everyday words. Like *everyday*.

This word, for example, is an adjective. If you noticed, I used it in an earlier sentence, and you may recall learning in school (way back when) that adjectives "describe a noun." So you would use *everyday* when describing everyday things. It's an everyday occurrence. These are everyday habits. Now, the word *every* is also an adjective, so how do you know when you need to break that word apart and use two words: *every day*?

The key is the word *day*. *Day* is a noun, so when you are talking about days and describing them (unless you are calling one "an everyday day"), you want to use two words. For example:

- Every day I walk the same street to work.
- I'm going every day to the market to get fresh fruit.
- I am counting every day until you arrive.

So now, think about the words anyone and any one. The same basic principle applies. Use anyone (pronoun) when you mean any person. Any is an adjective (unless you are using it as an adverb, as in "this doesn't help any"). So you would write:

- I could eat any one of those cookies.
- Any one of my friends might show up first.
- I think any one of those ten ideas would work.

But you would write:

- Is anyone home?
- Can anyone tell me where to go?
- I don't think anyone cares.

Well, when it comes to correct usage, I care.

EVERYDAY WORDS THAT ARE MISUSED EVERY DAY

A lot of the words we use have changed meaning over time, differing from their common or intended use. Some words sound so much like other words that they are often used interchangeably, like *bemused* and *amused*.

Here's a list of some everyday words that are often misused. See if you are guilty of misunderstanding the true meaning and usage of these words. If you are, don't feel bad. You're not alone.

- *Ironic*: It doesn't mean something funny or bad that's happened to you. It means the occurrence of something opposite to what you expect (although *irony* has a number of various meanings and applications). An example of an ironic situation: a domestic violence prosecutor being been charged with domestic violence.
- *Irregardless*: It's not a word, sorry. Use *regardless*. Regardless of what anyone tells you.
- *Peruse*: It does not mean to skim or browse over a bit of writing. It means to read something attentively (the opposite). Peruse originally comes from "per use," which traditionally indicates that you plan to "use up" the text with your passionate reading of it.
- *Consent*: It does not mean to give one's permission or agreement. It means to passively agree, even if you have a negative opinion of what you're agreeing to. If you consent to something, you're not cheering it on. You're allowing it to happen, with your permission.
- *Compelled*: It does not mean to voluntarily do something, usually out of a moral or internal impulse. It means to be forced, obligated, or pressured into doing something—the exact opposite of what you might think, and there's an easy way to see how. If you have to give "compulsory service" in the military, that means you don't have a choice. Compelled comes from "compulsory," so if you're "compelled" to give a truthful eye-witness testimony during a court case, that means you gotta do it.

I suppose it's a bit ironic for an editor to encourage the proper use of words when she might feel compelled to consent to her readers to peruse such a grammar book—irregardless of the fatuosity of the task. (No, fatuosity isn't a real word either.) Hmmm . . . did I just say what I think I said?

NOTES

NOTES

NOTES

FICTION "RULES"

WHEN IT COMES TO WRITING fiction, often there are no definitive rules to certain aspects of structuring sentences. In addition, a writer's voice, writing style, tone, and genre can and should influence choices in how to craft narrative, internal thinking, speech, and description.

Since this handy grammar guide is not a course in how to write fiction, I won't be delving into these topics. But there are some basic principles or practices that many fiction writers use, regardless of genre, to help them tighten up their writing and keep prose from becoming muddled, clunky, or redundant.

I mentioned this earlier in this book: One of my English teachers in high school had a saying he often repeated: "Say what you mean. Don't say what you don't mean." It's stuck with me for four decades, and I often think of this when writing. It may sound simple, but the advice is sage. The task of an adept writer is to figure out what she wants to say, then find the best way to say it.

Granted, when in a character's voice, the rules can often be set aside to convey the personality intended. Speech and thoughts may be grammatical wrong but entirely appropriate for that character due to his background, education, and other factors. But there are specific places where bending or breaking the established rules of grammar is not a good idea. Your novel or short story (or anything you write) should showcase a handle on correct grammar.

So be judicious with breaking the rules. And use your judgment in deciding when and if to follow these fiction "rules" I've presented here in this book. If some of them can help you write better, tighter sentences, then they'll have value for you. And if you think of others, jot them down in the Notes section.

STRONG NOUNS AND VERBS

I am a stickler for strong nouns and verbs. I got this bug from a college creative-writing teacher.

Perhaps the weakest sentence structure is one that begins with "it was" or "there were." So often when I critique a manuscript, I ask the question in the comment balloon: "What is *it*? Who are *they*?" This creative writing teacher I had decades ago had this as his mantra: "Strong nouns and verbs, strong nouns and verbs . . ." The mantra has stuck with me ever since.

So, go through your manuscript and search for *it was* and *there were* and replace each phrase with a strong noun and verb. Instead of "It was raining hard," try something more descriptive like "rain pelted the roof." I add to my list of weak words regularly, and I often use Word's Find feature to locate those weak words, then replace them with stronger ones.

I also have another chart of cool verbs I've come to love, and will often refer to it when I feel I need a better, more evocative verb than the one stuck in my head or hastily plunked down in my manuscript. Only few writers will get brownie points for starting their sentences with "It was a dark and stormy night." Even Snoopy got stuck on that first sentence (can you picture that *Peanuts* cartoon?)—no doubt because the noun and verb were so boring, he just could not get inspired to continue.

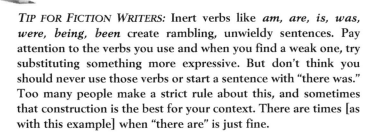

TIP FOR FICTION WRITERS: Inert verbs like *am, are, is, was, were, being, been* create rambling, unwieldy sentences. Pay attention to the verbs you use and when you find a weak one, try substituting something more expressive. But don't think you should never use those verbs or start a sentence with "there was." Too many people make a strict rule about this, and sometimes that construction is the best for your context. There are times [as with this example] when "there are" is just fine.

ARE YOU OVERLY PASSIVE?

Writers have heard a lot about avoiding passive voice or passive construction. Some are overly neurotic about this topic, making hard-and-fast rules that say you should never ever use the word *was* anywhere in your writing. But I disagree.

There are times when passive voice or the word *was* is the best choice. If your character is in the process of doing one thing when something else happens, you need to use the passive progressive structure: "I was stirring the noodles, when my contact fell into the water." That works perfectly. If you try to rewrite that to avoid the passive construction and come up with "I stirred the noodles as my contact fell in the water" it's a bit off.

Sure, writers often overuse the progressive tense ("was ___ing" or "is ___ing"). But there are times when it is just right. When the receiver of the action is more important than the doer, the passive voice is preferable and sometimes more effective.

In the passive voice, the subject and direct object are reversed, and this reversal can occur in any verb tense, for example:

- Tom watches football while the grass is cut by Sue. (Present tense)
- Tom watched football while the grass was cut by Sue. (Simple past tense)
- Tom is watching football while the grass is being cut by Sue. (Present progressive tense)
- Tom was watching football while the grass was being cut by Sue. (Past progressive tense)
- Tom has watched football while the grass has been cut by Sue. (Present perfect tense)
- Tom had watched football while the grass had been cut by Sue. (Past perfect tense)
- Tom will watch football while the grass will be cut by Sue. (Future tense)
- Tom will be watching football while the grass will be being cut by Sue. (Future progressive tense)

By using a more active voice, you will have a stronger, less wordy sentence. Why not just say "Tom watched football while Sue cut the grass"?

So don't be so strict with passive voice, yet think about using it only when it conveys the exact meaning you're after.

SPEAKER TAGS: YOU CAN'T COUGH SPEECH

I'm surprised by how often I see incorrect speaker tag verbs. Those are the verbs used to describe speech.

It's important to understand that speaker tags can *only* use verbs that can create speech. Writers often get creative with verbs in their speaker tags, but many are incorrectly used.

Wrong:

- "I love you," he smiled (or laughed, joked, lied, sighed, coughed, chuckled, etc.).

You can't sigh speech or cough speech, so only use verbs like *said, asked, replied.* Simpler is better. The word *said* is most recommended because it is considered invisible—the reader is so used to seeing that word that she glosses over it, which is a good thing.

There are simple ways to tweak your sentence to use a variation of the verb you want:

- "I love you," he said with a smile.
- "I love you." He coughed, then added, "I mean . . . I think I do."

Sometimes you can fudge this rule a bit. You might argue that a person can grumble or sigh words. I get your point, but technically you might sigh while you are saying words. And grumble is defined as "muttering in discontent." So since you can mutter words, you could probably say you grumble them as well. Just don't grumble at me.

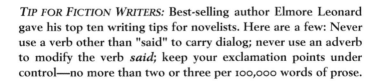

> *TIP FOR FICTION WRITERS:* Best-selling author Elmore Leonard gave his top ten writing tips for novelists. Here are a few: Never use a verb other than "said" to carry dialog; never use an adverb to modify the verb *said*; keep your exclamation points under control—no more than two or three per 100,000 words of prose.

DON'T GET FROWNED UPON

If you haven't heard it by now, adverbs are often frowned upon. It's true— a lot of beginning writers use adverbs excessively. And it does make your writing look cluttered and amateurish.

Why? Because it is better writing to have the choice of words and the structure of a sentence imply the mood, emotion, or intent of what you are trying to get across. Rather than tell that someone is angry ("Go away," he said angrily), show it ("Go away," he said, slamming the door in her face).

If you really feel you need to tell an emotion and you just want that adverb, try rewriting so you change the adverb into a noun. Instead of "He slammed the door angrily," write "He slammed the door in anger."

I would still leave out "anger" since slamming implies it. But if you are worried the reader might not get your emotional intent by the description alone, play around with the word you want to use.

Instead of "I have to leave," she said fearfully:

- "I have to leave," she said, fearful of his response.
- "I have to leave." Fear gripped her as she awaited his response.
- "I have to leave," she said, knowing the fear was evident on her face.

Still better would be to leave fear out of it completely and just show your character afraid—hands shaking, voice tremulous, throat constricted.

You don't need to get neurotic and take every adverb out of your book, but try to find other, more creative ways to get the emotion across without the dreaded "*ly.*"

TIP FOR Fiction *WRITERS:* Go through and find modifiers like *very, really, truly, actually,* and the like. If you've chosen the right word in your sentence to express the mood or effect you want, you won't need these words. Using modifier like these will defeat your purpose in writing a strong sentence.

THAT THAT MIGHT NOT BE THAT NECESSARY

"That that that that writer used is unnecessary . . ." Many of my clients will tell you I have a thing about "thats." Writers too often throw in a *that* for good measure, cluttering sentences with *that* word all too often. Much of the time you can take that *that* out.

Here are some instances where you can take *that* out:

- I said ~~that~~ she could come over.
- I hope ~~that~~ you will understand.
- I want to tell you ~~that~~ I love you.

Use *that* when you want to set something apart from something else:

- I want that donut—not the one with the sprinkles.
- Not everything that glitters is gold.

If you take that out and the meaning is confusing, keep it in. But at least try reading your line without it to see if that *that* is really ~~that~~ essential! That's all folks!

TIP FOR FICTION WRITERS: "A rambling, unwieldy sentence generally hangs from a weak verb," says Claire Cook in *Line by Line.* Verbs like *to be* and *to have* or *to exist* used extensively can weaken your writing and slow down the pace of your story. Find your long-winded sentences and see if you can spot that weak or vague verb, then replace it with a stronger one.

TIP FOR FICTION WRITERS: Be sure to set off direct address with a comma, whether it's a proper name or a generic term. Look at the difference in meaning between "Let's eat Grandpa" and "Let's eat, Grandpa." That comma placement is crucial. Also, use a pair of commas where needed. Example: "Hey, everyone, let's go."

A WORD YOU MAY HAVE NO NEED OF

One word you usually don't need is *of*. In my editing jobs, I spend almost as much time taking out *of* as I do that. You can take *of* out of all the sentences [not "all *of* the sentences"] below:

- I knew all ~~of~~ the people at the party.
- All ~~of~~ the answers flew out of my head.
- I know ~~of~~ some things we can do.
- We went outside ~~of~~ the house.
- I want to see you all ~~of~~ the time.

You want to keep *of* in places where you mean "pertaining":

- He spoke highly of his friend John.

Or when using the phrase "outside of":

- Outside of [with the exception of] a dog, a book is man's best friend.

> *TIP FOR FICTION WRITERS:* Wilson Follett (author of *Follett's Modern American* Usage) said, "Anyone who will struggles to reduce a hundred words to fifty without losing meaning will see looseness, inconsistency, and aberration vanish." Get in the habit of checking sentences one by one, omitting needless words and replacing weak ones with strong ones. You'll find over time that you write better and better, needing fewer rewrites.

> *TIP FOR FICTION WRITERS:* Try to avoid creating scenes in which the characters are sitting around drinking tea or coffee. Literary agent Donald Maass complains that this is the most overused scenario, and does not lend itself well for significant action to take place. Try to vary the locale of your scenes, if possible, to add interest and scope to your novel.

"YOU KNOW, BOB . . ."

For some reason, writers like to use a character's name often in dialog:

- "You know, Alice, I really like those shoes."
- "Really, Jane? I got them on sale last week."
- "Alice, that's great. Where'd you get them?"
- "I got them at Macy's, Jane."

The thing is, we rarely use a person's name in dialog with them. If you are calling someone's attention to you, yes, you will say their name, but listen to conversations and see if you can *ever* catch one person using the other's name. It almost never occurs. If you don't believe me, go to a coffee shop and listen in on conversations. Pay attention to how often your friends or family call you by your name when they're talking with you. You may be surprised.

So go through your sections of dialog in your novel and take out names everywhere you can. There may be places where they feel appropriate, but more often than not they are creating unnatural clunky dialog.

The same rule applies when using your character's name over and over in your narrative. Once the reader knows who you are talking about, you don't need to name John or Jane in every sentence. It can help to read your chapters aloud to catch those repeating names.

TIP FOR FICTION WRITERS: **The best way to get a clear sense of the euphony of your writing is to hear your work read back to you out loud. Not only will you hear if a sentence is wordy or clunky, you will catch repetitive words or phrases. If you read aloud to yourself, you often will miss those mistakes—because you know what you meant to say, so you often will edit or miss a word without really seeing the error on the page. It's best to buy a program like Natural Reader, which will read back to you. And it won't miss those sentences in which you wrote** *the the* **or** *she got in car.*

AM I BEING REDUNDANT OR WHAT?

Well, we all speak in redundancies and think nothing of it. Really—how many of us say "close proximity" or "major breakthrough"? (Is there any such thing as a minor breakthrough? Maybe.) Part of writing efficiently and concisely involves catching redundant or superfluous words or phrases that are really not needed. Here are some groups of words where either one or the other word will suffice by itself:

- adequate enough
- paramount importance
- past history (unless you're into sci-fi or some branch of quantum mechanics and want to distinguish from future history)
- serious danger (funny to me)
- total annihilation
- trained professional
- joint cooperation
- final outcome
- eliminate altogether

Maybe if we pay attention and look for redundancy, we can get rid of some of these unnecessary *habitual customs.*

TIP FOR FICTION WRITERS: Do you really need that modifier? Words like *very, really, truly,* and *actually* may only add bulk but no value to a sentence. A *very big* elephant could be a *huge* or *massive* elephant. Can you be *rather furious* or *fairly essential?* It reminds me of the line about being "a little pregnant." You either are or you aren't.

CIRCUMLOCUTION AT ITS BEST (OR WORST)

I love the word *circumlocution*. I never really have an opportunity to use it, so I'm creating one here. It means "the use of an unnecessarily large number of words to express an idea."

Writers should aim to avoid wordiness, but so many of us seem to just pack in those extraneous words into our sentences, which would read so much better if we chopped the bulk of them out and pared them down. I've come to love a nice, concise, clear sentence, and so I strive to trim away all that extra annoying fat (which is bad for you, right?).

Okay, if you didn't notice above (I sure hope you did!), I gave you two great examples of circumlocution. Let me rewrite those sentences here:

> Writers should aim to avoid wordiness, but many pack extraneous words into their sentences, which would be greatly improved if pared down. I've come to love a concise sentence, and so I strive to trim the fat. (I eliminated thirty out of sixty-seven words.)

Here are some phrases that can be reduced to a simpler expression:

- a large portion of (many)
- are in possession of (have)
- at this point in time (now)
- in spite of the fact that (although)
- in the not-too-distant future (soon)
- in the vicinity of (near)
- put in an appearance (appear)
- take into consideration (consider)
- made a statement saying (said, stated)

Think about reading through your manuscript with the idea of boiling down wordy phrases into the simplest form—like you did in that chemistry class in school (and didn't burn the Bunsen burner, I hope!). You may find that a goodly number of words (many) are far and beyond (more) than you absolutely must without fail have (need). Happy (succinct, tight) writing!

HE SAID, SHE SAID

Here's a worthy bit of advice—only use speaker tags when needed. Too many writers feel they have to put "he said" (or worse: "he quipped, interjected, exclaimed") every time any character says something. However, most of the time the reader knows who is speaking.

If you are writing a conversation with just two people, you only occasionally need to mention the speaker's name just to keep the reader clear on who's speaking. But alternating with a narrative tag instead is a good idea. Don't use both.

Wrong:

- John shook his head. "I wouldn't do that if I were you," he said.

Correct:

- John shook his head. "I wouldn't do that if I were you."

Be sure that when you do use an action (narrative tag) to identify who is speaking, you keep the action and speech together in the same paragraph to avoid confusion. Too often in the manuscripts I edit, I get confused as to who is speaking because the writer will put a line of speech on one line, then that character's action in the next paragraph along with a different character's speech.

> *TIP FOR FICTION WRITERS:* Break up long passages of dialog with beats. Beats are short bits of action or movement, such as a character walking to the sink or brushing hair out of her eyes. Try to make the beats purposeful and don't overdo them.

> *TIP FOR FICTION WRITERS:* It always sounds more natural to say "John said" rather than "said John." Unless you want to have an old-fashioned or stylized type of writing, which can be appropriate in fantasy novels or some historical fiction.

ONE THING LEADS TO ANOTHER

One thing I see a lot in manuscripts is two sequential events happening simultaneously. Authors often construct sentences like this:

- Turning the doorknob, she ran over and grabbed him and pushed him away.
- She stirred the cereal on the stove, sitting down with a sigh.
- Opening the car door, he turned on the ignition and started the car.
- He poured a cup of water, setting it down on the nightstand.

Certain things have to occur in sequence. You first turn the doorknob, then open the door, then grab the guy. You stir the cereal, then sit down and sigh (maybe you are sick of eating cereal?). After the man opens the car door, he then turns on the ignition and starts the car. Don't be afraid to use then. It's a useful word.

- I wrote this sentence, then went into the kitchen to get a cup of coffee.
- Not: I wrote this sentence, heading into the kitchen to get a cup of coffee.

Well, maybe if I balanced my laptop with one hand and typed with the other, I could manage to accomplish that feat.

Tip for Fiction Writers: Strunk and White say, "Omit needless words." Most writing experts agree less is more. If you have a clunky sentence and you're feeling it's not conveying exactly what you want it to mean, see if you can take out a few or half of the words. Chop one long sentence up into two and take out as many adverbs and adjectives as you can. See if that makes for clearer meaning.

SOME EXTRANEOUS WORDS THAT CLUTTER

I often find myself trimming down words when I do content edits for my clients. One author I know told me she went through one of her earlier manuscripts (she has more than a hundred published novels now) and deleted as many unnecessary speaker tags as she could find. She trimmed her word count down *six thousand* words!

So here are some words you can take out:

- He thought ~~to himself~~ [You can only think to yourself, so leave out those words. And if you use italics for thoughts in your novel, you often don't need to say "he thought" since it's clearly implied.]
- He stood, ~~up~~ then sat ~~down~~
- He nodded ~~his head~~
- Amid~~st~~, among~~st~~
- First~~ly~~, second~~ly~~, last~~ly~~
- Choose from ~~among~~ three choices [redundant]
- I don't like him, but ~~nevertheless~~ I'll go anyway [redundant so take out either *but* or *nevertheless*.]

TIP FOR FICTION WRITERS: If you write horror fiction, you might enjoy these humorous tips by author Edgar Allan Poe: "Employ an unreliable narrator, preferably one who doesn't know he is insane and has no recollection of such events as digging into a grave to rip out the teeth of his recently departed lover. Use grandiloquent words, such as *heretofore, forthwith,* and *nevermore.* A little Latin will also enhance the text. When in doubt, bury someone alive." I hope you can tell he's being a bit cynical.

POP GOES THE WEASEL (WORD)

I thought I would give you a partial list of my "weasel words." These are words I overuse and are often unnecessary and clutter up my books. I will go through, usually when done with my first draft, and do a "find" for these words and destroy them! (Although, sometimes I do need one and after much deliberation will vet it and allow it to remain.)

You should come up with your own list, but I bet some of your words are the same as mine.

One way to learn what your weasel words are is to ask your critique partner or writing group to point them out to you. Invariably, we cannot see some our own. I have often muttered to myself: "I can't believe I used that word again!" In addition to weasel words, you may have pet phrases you need to shed, like "rolled her eyes."

Okay, here's my list. Make a list of yours on the blank Notes page at the end of this section.

- just
- have to
- that
- could
- would
- began to
- started to
- it; it was
- there was
- were
- very
- rather
- some
- thought
- wondered
- mused
- had
- -ly [to find adverbs]
- -ing [to find progressive construction]

ACT FIRST, TALK LATER

Here's something I see a lot in manuscripts, and although it's not a strict rule, it's just something to consider when tweaking your sentence structure to make the writing flow more smoothly.

It's very possible you may mean for some action to be happening before a character's

speech, but if you place it after the speech, it will feel like the character stops speaking, then acts. So unless sequence in time requires otherwise, always try to put action before speech.

Wrong:

- "I knew you were going to say that." John sighed and slapped the table.

Correct:

- John sighed and slapped the table, "I knew you were going to say that."

If the speech spurs on an action, then you'll want to put it after the speech:

- "I can do that in a split second!" Cindy snapped her fingers in Bill's face, then marched out the door.
"You're leaving me?" Tears filled Ann's eyes as she slapped John's cheek. "Then get out!" She put her hands on her hips and mustered the meanest scowl she could, refusing to buckle while John backed out the door.

TIP FOR FICTION WRITERS: Conventional dictionaries don't have the space to explain all the different shades of meaning for every word, and fiction writers sometimes create their own with metaphor and creative prose. But before you start tweaking the meaning of a word, be sure to look it up and understand its various uses. A grammar book that explores "confusables" is helpful in getting a deeper look at the meaning of words.

NOTES

NOTES

NOTES

INDEX

ABOUT THE AUTHOR

C. S. LAKIN IS THE AUTHOR of more than a dozen novels in various genres. She works full-time as a professional copyeditor and writing coach specializing in manuscript critiques. When she's not editing or writing, she loves to teach workshops and lead critique teams at conferences around the US.

Her award-winning blog Live Write Thrive is dedicated to instructing and encouraging writers at all stages of their writing journey. Along with offering tips and insights on marketing, self-publishing, and strategic planning, she creates a year-long course each year with a different focus, specific for novel writers. Her Say What? section gives lighthearted and simplified grammar tips with the aim of making grammar a fun and painless subject to learn. This book comprises three years of blog posts from this section on Live Write Thrive, and was compiled and put in book form due to repeated request from readers.

Lakin is currently writing a sweet Western historical romance series (under the pen name Charlene Whitman). The first book, *Colorado Promise*, ran up the best-seller charts within weeks and is soon to be followed in 2014 by *Colorado Hope* and *Colorado Dream*. She also plans to release two other writing craft books sometime in 2014 based on the first two year-long courses that ran on her blog: *Writing the Heart of Your Story* and *Shoot Your Novel*.

You can follow Lakin on Twitter via
@cslakin, and @livewritethrive,
and on Facebook at
http://www.facebook.com/c.s.lakin.author.
Learn about her critique services at
http://www.critiquemymanuscript.com.
Subscribe to Live Write Thrive and improve both your grammar and writing skills!

http://www.livewritethrive.com.

19127243R00133

Made in the USA
Middletown, DE
08 April 2015